To the memory of my beloved grandmother,
Rivka Berenson, who showed me the way.

# Nili Portugali

# The Act of Creation and the Spirit of a Place

## A Holistic-Phenomenological Approach to Architecture

**Edition Axel Menges**

© 2006  Edition Axel Menges, Stuttgart/London
ISBN 3-936681-05-8

Printing and binding: Everbest Printing Co., Ltd, China

Editorial supervision: Nora Krehl-von Mühlendahl
Design: Nili Portugali

अंबष्ठ

# Contents

*Nili Portugali,
watercolor,
1981, seminar
on colors,
University of
California,
Berkeley.*

# A personal note

I am a practicing architect working in Israel for more than 30 years, and a lecturer at the Bezalel Academy of Art & Design, Department of Architecture, Jerusalem. My work has focused on both practice and theory, and is tightly connected to the Phenomenological-Holistic School of Thought.

Hereby I would like to note those milestones in my biography which have left their stamp on my architectural work. These include the various sources of knowledge I have been exposed to in my formal architectural studies, and their linkage to the streams of thought that had been developing in architecture at the time, my studies of Buddhist philosophy, and most important of all – the place I grew up in, my heritage and roots.

My curiosity about what lies behind the order of human and organic architecture, which has the enormous power to excite us, and which is endowed with beauty and soul, and my willingness to understand, were born when I was a first year student of architecture in the Technion Institute of Technology in Haifa, Israel, at the end of the 1960s. This was also the start of my search for the processes by which these buildings were created, a search which continued through my studies at the Architectural Association School of Architecture (AA) in London (diploma 1973) and my post-graduate studies in architecture and Buddhist philosophy at University of California, Berkeley (1979–81) and my work with Prof. Christopher Alexander at the Center for Environmental Structure in Berkeley (1979–81).

My intuitive feeling was that what lies behind those places and buildings where we have a deep emotional experience that goes far beyond their basic usefulness, is a truth, facts and reasons I wanted to understand and act upon in my design work.

The late 1960s and early 1970s brought to the forefront of science in general and architecture in particular the quantitative methodological approach, as presented in Geoffrey Broadbent's book, *Design in Architecture, Architecture and the Human Sciences* (John Wiley & Sons, 1973). According to this theory, the creative process is a product of quantitative planning methods, where complex relationships between man and his environment are defined by matrixes and formulas. I adopted this logical and systematic working process, which enabled me to identify and separate the various elements of a building required by the

*Nili Portugali, construction experiment, 1969, Technion, Haifa.*

program and combine them to a whole. This resulted in plans that on the conventional level were indeed neat, reasoned and coherent. The projects that grew out of this basically mechanistic methodology met the physical and social needs of their users, but only partially answered their *emotional and spiritual* needs. In other words, this methodology was not aimed to create buildings with a *soul*.

When in the early 1970s I left the Technion and pursued my studies at the AA in London, I found a school where the main theme in teaching architecture was conceptual, in line with the conceptual-art tendency first displayed at that time in an exhibition at the ICA gallery (in London) under the name *When Attitudes Become Form*, an exhibition that became a landmark in the history of contemporary art. In discussions held at that time in the AA by mainstream followers, man's environment was conceived as a mere metaphor for science fiction, completely ignoring and even belittling anyone who tried to speak about the *emotional-human experiential* relations between man and place.

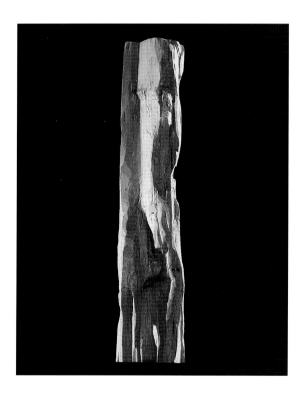

This approach was advanced by earlier as well as later movements, such as the Archigram in London, the post-modernist stream on the east coast of the US and the deconstructivist stream still starring today. These movements, although different from each other, have one thing in common and that is their basic assumption that there is no absolute truth behind architecture and that beauty and comfort are subjective concepts that have to do with style, fashion and the personal vision of the creator. In fact this assumption denied any objective public discussion on the definition of beautiful architecture.

I kept searching for a way to design new towns, villages, buildings or gardens with the same *soul* and heart-touching quality we experience in the various places we really love and want to come back to again and again. I took photos and tried to record and understand the visible structures of those organic places, using them as a model for the new projects I planned. The outcome made me understand that no place is independent of the reality to which it belongs, and that planning a new environment with that desired quality involves not just an application of an existing model, but a deep understanding of the *rules and processes* that led to its creation. When I completed

*Nili Portugali, 3D design (wood), 1969, Technion, Haifa.*

*Nili Portugali, 3D design (plaster), 1969, Technion, Haifa.*

*Nili Portugali,*
*drawings, 1969,*
*Technion, Haifa.*

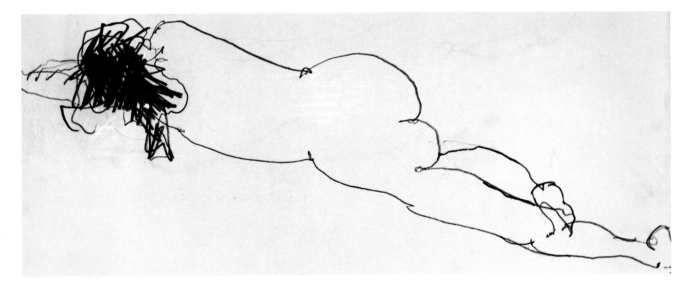

my studies and returned to Israel (1973), my first commission was planning the house of the writer David Shutz in Jerusalem. The planning process in this case, unlike the conventional ones I have been taught which took place on the drawing board in the office and were transferred to the site, took place *on the site itself*. I sat there for long hours, trying to feel and experience it first-hand. Each planning decision regarding the location and shape of the various rooms taken as a result of that experience was marked by red chalk on the ground. These marks were later recorded on paper to become the building plan. But even in this case, where the house clearly grew out of the reality on its site, the critical question still left open was, what are the *rules and processes* that determine the right spatial *relations* between the various parts of the building, namely, what is the secret of harmony in architecture.

*Shutz residence, Jerusalem, 1978. The boundaries of the new house were dictated by the chalk marks, which recorded the planning decisions taken previously on the site itself.*

My work with Prof. Christopher Alexander in the late 1970s and early 1980s at the Center for Environmental Structure in Berkeley, and my close study of his work and research, made me realize, this time in a clear and implementable way, what lies behind the harmony in architecture and what operative processes lead to its creation.

My acquaintance with the holistic approach in general through my study of Buddhist philosophy in Berkeley and twenty years later with the teachings of His Holiness the Dalai Lama, and with its application to architecture in particular, brought me back to the physical and spiritual experience I had in the Kabalist city of Safad (Israel), birthplace and hometown of my family (Berenson) for seven generations. This experience influenced more than anything my conception and vision of how a place should feel.

The city of Safad, dated to the period of the second temple and haven to thousands of Jews who fled from Spain and Portugal in fear of the Inquisition, became in the 16th century the most important spiritual center of the Jewish community of Eretz Israel. Many of the Jews who settled there were prominent mysticists and scholars of religious law and *Kabala*, including Rabbi Shimon Bar Yochai, who is thought to be the author of the *Zohar*, one of the most important Kabalistic texts, and Rabbi Yosef Karo, author of *Shulchan Aruch* (code of laws). The doctrine of *Kabala*, which includes various interpretations of the essence of divinity, the creation, mysticism, reincarnation etc., undoubtedly affected the unique physical structure of Safad. The patterns of its architectural language, including the colors that brighten the

*The Tree of Wishes, Safad cemetery. According to Jewish tradition, before making a wish one should circle the tree seven times.*

*Safad.*

*Ben Avraham residence, Zichron. The architypical patterns of an entrance courtyard and an entrance gate derived their final version from the physical context of the site.*

city, were based on sources of knowledge drawn from the *Kabala* or from the writings of Maimonides, a tradition dated to the 16th century. Thus, for example, the light blue, blue and white colors used to paint houses, gates and tombstones symbolized the colors of the *Zohar* and of divinity in the *Kabala*. The courtyards and gates at the entrance to the houses separated them from the street, while those at the entrance to the synagogues separated the holy from the secular.

*A traditional pattern of an entrance courtyard, Safad.*

*A traditional pattern of a main-entrance gate, Safad.*

Alexander's research on the pattern language and the nature of order of places endowed with feeling made me understand that beyond the subjective effect the city of Safad had and still has on me there is an *ultimate truth* common to us all as human beings. Thus the use I make of the pattern language I absorbed in Safad in the process of my architectural creations has its source not only in nostalgia or my love for the place, but in a scientifically explainable, universal phenomenon. These patterns to which I had been exposed left their stamp on me, and later became, if unconsciously, the vocabulary of my architectural language. These same patterns, in their junction with the changing conditions of the site and the programmatic contexts, naturally produced new projects, *different from each other in form*, but *similar in the human feeling* they projected, as will be described in this book.

*Light blue and blue are the colors of the Zohar and of divinity in the Kabala. Safad.*

*Nili Portugali, watercolor, 1980, seminar on colors, University of California, Berkeley.*

*Nili Portugali,*
*watercolor,*
*1980, seminar*
*on colors,*
*University of*
*California,*
*Berkeley.*

16

# Preface

The aim of this book is to present the interpretation given in architecture to the holistic-organic worldview, a worldview which stands in recent years at the forefront of the scientific discourse as a whole (in disciplines like cosmology, neurobiology, psychology, particle physics and brain sciences, and is linked to recent theories of complexity), and is tightly related to the fundamentals of Buddhist philosophy, and my particular interpretation of it in both theory and practice, in projects I designed and built in Israel.

The first part of the book presents the various elements of this approach and describes the planning process stemming from it, a process striving towards phenomenological architecture that generates a spiritual experience common to all people, no matter where or from what culture they come from. The second part demonstrates how this approach, as well as the unique planning process, a process *fundamentally* different from conventional ones, were implemented in a variety of public and private projects, on different levels of scale, in relation to the physical, cultural and social reality of the place they were planned and built on. This reality includes both the specific context of the project and the site and the wide context of Israel as a unique interface between the orient and the west. A cultural interface I personally represent, being on mother's side a seventh generation descendent of the Berenson family, living in the Galilean city of Safad since the early 19th century, and on father's side granddaughter of Nisan Kahan one of the founders and guiding lights of the Zionist movement in Hungary.

Believing that beauty and harmony of any artifact are directly related to abstract geometrical properties inherent in the structure itself, and to the process by which they have created, led me to understand that creating a book – the task I undertook – is basically not different from planning a town square, a building or a piece of furniture. The same set of rules which determines the right relations between the parts and the whole and gives the sense of unity in architecture applies in its abstract definition to anything consisting of material, form and color, on any level of scale. The difference lies in the components and complexity of the product. Thus, the line of thought and the work process which guide my architectural practice guided me in designing this book. For example, the choice of the grid and the type of fonts is analogous to the choice of a pattern language as the first step in the planning process of a building. The relative volume of and the right relations between the text, the illustrations and the void on the page of a book are analogous to the relative volume of and relations between the various elements in the built environment. The void which is necessary for breathing that we find both in nature and in any artifact endowed with beauty and soul, which provides physical and mental relief from the more intensive parts in any structure, like the park in the city, the courtyards in a building complex, or the living room in a private house is that part on a book paged void of text or pictures.

I hope that by presenting an approach which tries to identify those objective universal codes and needs common to us all as human beings, codes that cross cultures and link them together in harmony, and at the same time show a planning process which structurally responds to the identity of each cultural and social group we build for and to the uniqueness of each site, I will contribute something towards replacing current conceptions and approaches whereby aggressive political motives, arbitrary fashions and egotistical ambitions create the kind of architecture that forms a real threat to the physical and human environment we live in.

ऊंबुबक

# The architectural concept
# and its implementation

# Architecture is made for people.
# A phenomenological approach to
# architecture

The purpose of architecture, as I see it, is first and foremost to create a *human* environment for *human beings*. Buildings affect our lives and the fate of the physical environment in which we live over the course of many years, and therefore their real test is the test of time. The fine old buildings and places we always want to return to – those with timeless relevance – are the ones that touch our hearts, and have the power to create a deep and direct *emotional* experience.

Contemporary architecture as well as conceptual art sought to dissociate themselves from the world of *emotions* and connect the design process to the world of *ideas*, thus creating a rational relation between building and man, *devoid of any emotion*.

There are different ways to describe buildings that have this timeless quality, buildings that convey an inherent spiritual experience. Frank Lloyd Wright called them "the ones which take you beyond words". Quoted by Stephen Grabow, Christopher Alexander says: "The buildings that have spiritual value are a diagram of the inner universe, or the picture of the inner soul." And in *The Timeless Way of Building* Alexander writes: "There is one timeless way of building. It is thousands of years old, and the same today as it has always been. The great traditional buildings of the past, the villages and tents and temples in which man feels at home, have always been made by people who were very close to the center of this way. And as you will see, this way will lead anyone who looks for it to buildings which are themselves as ancient in their form as the trees and hills, and as our faces are."

Although this timeless quality exists in buildings rooted in different cultures and traditions, the experience they generate is common to all people, no matter where or from what culture they come from.

*Delphi, Greece: the Tholos (4th century BC).*

*Hsi-an-Fu, China: the Great Gander Pagoda (7th to 8th centuries).*

*Safad, Israel: Yosef Karo Synagogue (16th century).*

Thus Alexander's basic assumption was that behind this quality, which he calls "the quality without a name", lies a *universal* and eternal element *common to us all as human beings.*

The real challenge of current architectural practice is indeed to make the best use of the potential inherent in the modern technological age we live in while fulfilling the timeless needs common to us all as *human beings* in order to create a *friendly* environment. Needs that modern architecture in general has knowingly denied for the past 60 years.

The basic argument presented here is that in order to change the feeling of the environment and create places and buildings that we really feel part of and want to live in, what is needed is not a change of style, but a transformation of the *worldview* underlying current thought and approaches.

*A place with a spirit: a senior-citizens day center, Tel Aviv.*

# The holistic approach to architecture.
# The relation between the parts and the whole

The dissociation created in our time between man and his environment is a clear expression of the change that occurred in the concept that man is part of nature and not superior to it.

Comparing planning processes which resulted in dissociating man from his environment to planning processes that make him feel part of the physical world he lives in, emphasizes the difference between the *mechanistic-fragmentary* worldview and the *holistic-organic* one, which guides the *holistic school of thought* to which my own work belongs.

These are *two different sets of orders*.

The mechanistic worldview underlying contemporary architecture separates elements and creates an environment of autonomous fragments. The result are cities like Brasilia, Chandigarth, the satellite towns in England and the new neighborhoods around Jerusalem, where the structured disconnection between the house and the street, the street and the neighborhood, the neighborhood and the city arouses a feeling of detachment and alienation.

The holistic-organic approach that has been for many years at the forefront of the scientific thought in general and as implemented in my architectural work in particular regards the socio-physical environment as a system or a *dynamic whole*, the existence of which depends on the proper, ever-changing interrelations among the parts. Moreover, the creation and *existence* of each part *depend* on the *interrelations* between that part and the system.

His Holiness the Dalai Lama claims that understanding these expressions of dependent arising, cause and condition and cause and effect is condition for the realization of emptiness, being the foundation of all Buddhist teaching. In his book *The Joy of Living and Dying in Peace* he writes: "The teaching of dependent arising has vast implications. In general, everything comes into existence in dependence on other factors and conditions. ... Since things arise and come into existence in accordance with their causes, the Buddhist scriptures contain no presentation of a self. When we accept that everything is conditional, it is logical that we cannot accept an independent creator of the universe … and that any entity has an intrinsic existence that come into existence independently of many factors ..." He goes on in saying: "Everything that is composed from parts, or conditioned by causes and conditions, is impermanent and fleeting. Things do not stay forever. They continually disintegrate. This kind of 'subtle impermanence' is confirmed by scientific findings in disciplines like cosmology, neurobiology, psychology, and particle physics, disciplines that are the result of generations of scientific investigations. Their findings are closely related to Buddhist teachings."

In any organic system, each element has its own uniqueness and power, but always acts as part of a larger entity to which it belongs and which it complements. Having adopted this concept, I do not regard urban design, architecture, interior design and landscape design as independent disciplines removed from each other, but as *one continuous and dynamic system.* Thus the building is not perceived as a collection of *designed* fragments, but as *one hierarchical language,* in which every design detail, on any level of scale, is derived from the larger whole to which it belongs, which it seeks to enhance, and for whose existence it is responsible. *The overall feeling of inner wholeness and unity in a building thus stems from the proper inter-relations among its parts.*

The same idea is found in the Mandala, a model that represents processes occurring in nature, where there is always a center of energy feeding the parts around it. However, the very existence of this center of energy is dependent on the existence of the parts around it.

*Mandala of Durgatipari Sodhana.*

This concept of *interdependence and continuity* was presented in a public talk given by His Holiness the Dalai Lama, in which he noted: "The construction of the whole is caused continually by the disintegration of its parts. For example, the butter lamp as a whole is a source of light due to the melting of the butter. The melting of the butter is caused due to the heat produced by the lamp."

*The square, the building and the interior are one continuous sys-tem. Music cen-ter and library in Tel Aviv.*

# The planning process itself

### 1. Choosing a pattern language for the project

Based on the assumption that beauty and harmony are objective properties related to the geometrical properties inherent in the structure itself, and that feelings have to do with facts, Alexander states in his book *The Timeless Way of Building* that all places of organic order that seem unplanned and orderless are a clear expression of order on a deep and complex level. This order is based on absolute rules that have always determined the quality and beauty of a place, and is the source of the good feeling in it. In other words, there is a direct connection between the *patterns of events* that occur in a place and the physical patterns – *patterns of space* in his terminology – that constitute it.

The fact that places that share a common pattern of events (for example, Piazza San Marco in Venice and Piazza Mayor in Madrid), although different in form, all create the *same emotional pleasant experience*, gave rise to the hypothesis, that beyond what *appears different*, there is something else, common to them all.

This assumption led Alexander to an empirical research conducted at *The Center for Environmental Structure* in Berkeley, California, the aim of which was to analyze all those places in order to identify this common element. The basic assumption was that just as every substance has a basic component called an atom, the man-made environment consists of "atoms" he called patterns. Each pattern is an archetype of a structure that repeats itself in an infinite variety, and although form varies from place to place, there is an underlying structure that remains the same.

Let us take for example the pattern called *arcade* – an archetype of a structure that relates to the transition area between a building and the open space around it. Although the arcade in the Hadera synagogue is different from the one in the Assisi cloister or the one in the Tel Aviv senior-citizens day center, there is *one superstructure* common to them all, a superstructure that defines the *relationship* between the building and its surroundings. These pat-

*The Maimonides Central Sephardic Synagogue, Hadera.*

*Senior-citizens day center in Tel Aviv.*

*San Francesco, Assisi.*

terns, 250 in number, as listed in Alexander's book *A Pattern Language*, constitute a system that generates an entire language.

It includes patterns from the city level of scale to that of individual buildings and construction details. Each pattern in the language consists of other smaller patterns and at the same time is part of a larger pattern. In other words, each pattern is a *pattern of relationship*. The language is a generative one and the hierarchical order of the patterns it consists of is determined by the rules of the language itself. For example, if we take the pattern called *covered walkway,* the function of which in the larger system is to connect buildings, an entire set of smaller patterns – the height of the roof, the distance between the columns, the building materials, etc. – will immediately emerge and help to create it.

*The covered walkway is a pattern of relationships. It helps to connect buildings and is generated by the harmony of its details.*

Since the environment consists of patterns that produce a common experience, the relevant question was, what lies behind the *specific patterns* that produce the same *comfortable feeling* we all share in that environment. The explanation was, that as in the various spoken languages there is, according to Chomsky, a common structural element he calls the language of languages or the underlying patterns, an element that is *innate in human beings* and therefore common to us all (which explains why children can so easily learn a foreign language), so in the physical space there are patterns that reflect an *innate pattern structured in our brain*.

*The first step* in the planning process is to determine the patterns of space that are relevant to the project. Some of them will stem from the specific context of the project and the cultural reality of the place, patterns that vary from place to place, and some from the more basic needs common to us all as human beings wherever we are.

*"It is the network of connections between patterns which creates the language."*
*The Timeless Way of Building (p. 314).*

As in any organic system, where the genetic codes regulate not only the functioning of the cell but its relations to the organism as a whole, in this generative pattern language the hierarchy of the patterns and the interrelations between them stem from the rules of the language. Once I have decided on the list of patterns relevant to a specific project, a set of interrelations is automatically created between them, organically defining the scheme of the project. This scheme is then translated into a plan.

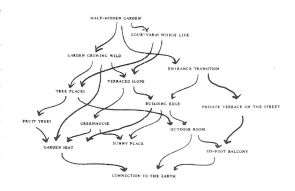

## 2. Planning on the site itself.
## A transformational planning process

The plan of the building that is finally created is actually a structure of balance between the abstract pattern language chosen for the project and the *living reality of the actual site*, a reality that *differs* from site to site.

The planning process proposed here is *fundamentally* different from the common planning processes. Once I have set a list of patterns for the project, all planning decisions concerning the physical structure of the project are taken literally *on the site itself*. Unlike the common planning process, where planning takes place in the office and is then transferred to the site, here the drawings are merely the *recording* of those planning decisions taken *on the site itself.*

Organic architecture should not be conceived as a personal and arbitrary vision of the architect, but as a product of the *actual reality* acting on the site, independent of us personally. The process of creation has to be inspired by what is *already there,* and our task as artists or architects is to discover, identify and revive those visible and hidden forces.

His Holiness the Dalai Lama refers in his book *The Joy of living and Dying in Peace* to that reality by saying: "One aspect of the process is first to know that things have a natural and innate mode of existence ... Reality is not something that the mind has fabricated anew. Therefore, when we search for the meaning of truth, we are searching for reality, for the way things actually exist.This is called the logic of suchness, which means that we investigate things on the basis of their suchness or nature. ... We need to be able to distinguish between the mere clarity of the mind and those aspects that appear when extraneous factors such as attachment arise."

*Planning decisions taken on the site materialize in the building itself.*

27

The creative process which feeds on what is apparently already there, is definitely not a passive one. Unlike the common planning process, where everything is predetermined, this is a process whereby the plan of the building develops gradually from the interaction of the abstract planning patterns and the *unpredictable* developing situation on the site. This is a process that *frees* us from arbitrary preconceived images stored in the mind that are irrelevant to the evolution of the plan, and *opens a way* to *new things*.

In his book *Zen in the Art of Archery* Eugene Herrigel describes the *state of mind* in which the process of creation must take place: "Drawing the bow and loosing the shot happens independently of the archer. The hands must open like the skin of a ripe fruit. The archer must let himself go, to the point that the only thing that is left of him is a *purposeless* tension. ... At this state of mind, being *released from all attachments*, art should be practiced."

Each planning decision is the product of a direct experience of all the forces acting on the site, including the directions of the light and the view, the buildings and roads around, the topographical structure of the land, etc. The decisions are taken *intuitively*, since intuition is the only means of experiencing the environment *as a whole entity.*

The order according to which the planning decisions are taken on the site is determined by the hierarchical order in which the planning patterns appear on my list governed by the rules of the pattern language itself. Decisions are first made on issues that affect the larger scale we have to confront at any given moment along the development of the plan, moving to other decisions generating from them. Moreover, the planning process is not conceived as an additive, but rather as a *differentiating* one, where each new element of the plan is *differentiated* gradually from previous ones. Each decision taken on the site and marked on the ground actually *changes the configuration of the site as a whole.* That new whole (configuration) that has been created and can be fully visualized on the site forms the basis for the next decision. Since each stage is based on the previous one, a wrong decision creates a faulty system that cannot serve as a basis for the next decision.

The final "layout" that emerges on the site is measured and recorded by a surveyor. That moment when all the marks suddenly become *a whole,* a visible plan, is a moment of surprise and excitement. Experience has taught me that decisions which may sometimes appear irregular and strange on paper, often make sense in reality (where it comes from), and vice versa, a plan that appears perfect on paper (where it was created) may seem senseless on the site. So, if when looking at the "stakes plan" doubts arise concerning one or more of the decisions taken on the site, the correction is not made on paper in the office, but checked again *on the site itself.* The final "stakes plan" forms the basis for the final plan.

*Students of Nili Portugali practicing a design process on the site itself.*

# An illustration of a piecemeal process taking place on the site itself. Memorial Site for the Fallen Intelligence Servicemen

## Step 1. Identifying the natural focal points on the site

The location of each center is determined when that spot on the site that has the necessary qualities for the specific activity is found.

*1. A memorial corner located at the most intimate spot – at the far end of the site.*

*2. Outdoor assembly square located at the open area.*

*3. Outdoor sitting corners located in-between the trees.*

*4. Eucalyptus corner – a beautiful area around the trees.*

## Step 2. Identifying the main and secondary entrances to the site

"Place the main entrance of the building at a point where it can be seen immediately from the main avenues ..." (Quotation from the pattern *main-entrance gate*)

*The main entrance, clearly visible from the main road, was located at the spot that allows an overall view of the site.*

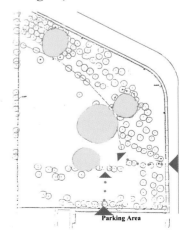

29

## Step 3. Linking the different activity centers marks the layout of the paths

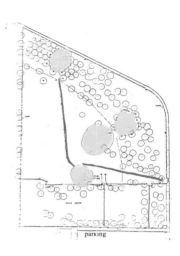

*The path that leads to the memorial corner.*

## Step 4. Marking the exact boundaries of each activity center and choosing the proper place for entering that center

*Eucalyptus corner.*

*Outdoor assembly square.*

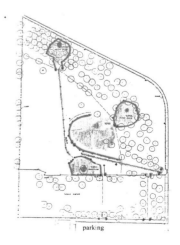

*Memorial corner.*

## Step 5. Marking the location of the built areas and building lines

"Buildings must always be built on those parts of the land which are in the worst condition, not the best ..." (Quotation from the pattern *site repair*)

The least pleasant parts of the site were chosen for the built area, while the best areas were left open.

*The beautiful areas, including the grove, were left undisturbed.*

## Step 6. Outlining in detail the plan for the outdoor activity areas and paths and identifying the focal points of each activity center

"Outdoor spaces which are merely 'left over' between buildings will, in general, not be used ..." (Quotation from the pattern *positive outdoors space*)

The outdoor spaces that are in-between the buildings were positively defined by the wings of the buildings, the arcades and the trellised walks around them.

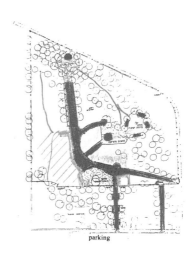

*The outdoor spaces were positively defined by the wings of the buildings, the arcades and the trellised walks around them.*

parking

31

## Step 7. The layout of the indoor spaces

"Buildings which displace natural light as the major source of illumination are not fit places to spend the day ..." (Quotation from the pattern *wings of light*)

The building is split into long and narrow wings, allowing the natural light to penetrate into all the floor areas.

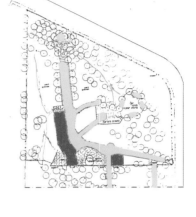

*The location of the different rooms inside the designated built area, in relation to the predetermined location of the outdoor activity centers.*

*A sketch drawing, recording the planning decisions taken on the site and marked on the ground.*

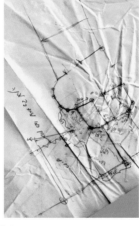

*The final stakes plan forms the basis for the final plan.*

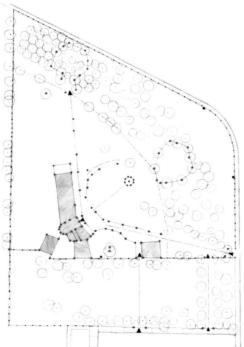

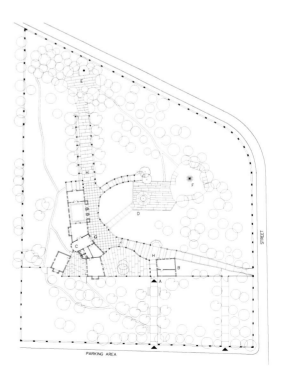

# The beauty is in the detail.
# The detail – pure functionalism derived from the whole

The secret enfolded in the beauty of a building (or of any artifact) as a whole lies in its spatial order and in the nature of its details. The details, like furniture, lighting accessories, materials and colors, are regarded as an *inherent part* of the building and therefore are an *inseparable* part of my planning process. The similarity in form between the details stems from the *common whole* to which they belong.

In modern society, beauty has become a term of abuse, often associated with inefficiency, impracticality, lack of functionalism and high costs. That notion of beauty is true when it relates to details as decorative elements and ornamentation *for its own sake.*

The Shakers, a religious sect that created an abundance of useful furniture and utensils in the mid-eighteenth century, noted that the wholeness and beauty of form are products of pure functionalism, and that there is no room for beautiful forms that do not flow from a

*functional* need. Take, for example, the gold-leaves capital of the iron column, which connects it to the beam. This part is functionally separate from the other parts of the column and was *therefore given a different form and color.* At the same time, however, the Shakers did not interpret the term "pure functionalism" in the *narrow* sense of the word, as did the modernists, for whom the expression "form follows function" was semantically connected only to the *physical* body of the building. They understood it in the broad sense, connecting it both to the physical and *spiritual* experience in a building. This is the experience I want to create for the users of the buildings I design.

*Music center and library in Tel Aviv.*

*The beautiful form of the water gutters stems from its function.*

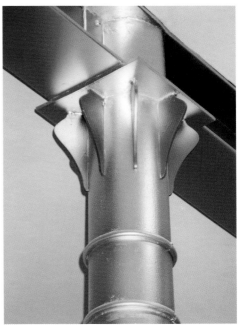

33

# Choosing the colors for the building

Choosing the colors for the building is one of the more difficult decisions in the design process. The choice of colors has an overwhelming effect on the feeling of the building. Colors have the power to give life and enhance the qualities inherent originally in a building or to suppress them. The choice of color is made intuitively *on the site* once the building is *completed*, a time when I can fully sense its mass within its immediate surrounding environment. I try to envision the colors (hues) that practically reveal themselves naturally from the building. Only then do I experiment with applications of those colors in order to arrive at the final tones.

As in the planning of the building, so at this stage of choosing the colors, the process is a gradual one. First I determine the color of the walls – the large mass, and then, in relation to that previous decision, follows the decisions about the colors of the window frames, the rails, the gates and all the other smaller details that complement, enhance and enlighten those previously chosen colors. In the example shown below the color chosen for the exterior walls, was the hue of the golden leaves that fell at that time of the year on the site.

*The color chosen for the exterior wall was the hue of the golden leaves that fall outside the building in autumn.*

*Ohel Shem community and school library, Ramat Gan.*

34

# A dialogue between the qualities of tradition and modern technology

Modern technology available today should not be conceived as an aim or a value in itself, but as a *tool* to create *a human and friendly* environment that will satisfy the basic needs common to all of us as *human beings*. Despite the unlimited possibilities it opens to us, technology should be used in a controlled, value-oriented and moral way.

*Senior-citizens day center in Tel Aviv.*

One of the immediate questions I am asked in reaction to the buildings I design is whether it is a new design that tries to reconstruct an architectural language of the past. My answer to that is that I do not attempt or aim to reconstruct the past or to nostalgically trace this or that style. The similarity and the *association* created between the buildings I design and those we know from the past, and the similar experience and feeling they create, originate in my use of the same fundamental *patterns* and planning codes that guided in the past, and will continue to guide in the future, in any culture and tradition, those who aspire to give a building *spirit and soul*, codes that have been brutally ignored (in general) by contemporary architecture, and which I try to revive in the buildings I design, in relation to the physical and social context of the place I am working in.

*A traditional pattern of an entrance gate in Safad.*

*The use of the pattern "entrance gate": senior-citizens day center in Tel Aviv; Ben Avraham residence, Zichron-Yaakov.*

*A traditional pattern of an entrance court-yard. Haari Ashkenazic Synagogue, Safad.*

*The use of the pattern "entrance court-yard": Hibat-Zion Synagogue, Jerusalem.*

35

# Selected buildings and projects

*Public buildings*
*Residential and mixed developments*
*Master plans*
*Private houses*

# *Public buildings*

# Music center and library

**Tel Aviv, Israel**
**Completion date: 1997**

## A unique dialogue between a new building and the historical environment

Preserving the spirit of a historical environment does not necessarily mean a fanatic repetition of its language. The Bialik district at the heart of Tel Aviv, with Bialik Square at its center, is a micro-document of the architectural history of Tel Aviv from the 1920s, the "eclectic period", when European architecture was brought to Israel and integrated with the local oriental architecture, to the 1930s and the new "International Style" somewhat later.

The new Music center and library built at Bialik Square (1997) is located on the site of a three-story residential house built in 1931 and demolished in 1994. My commission was to design a new building integrating a reconstructed part of the façade of the old one.

My conception was that once you demolish a building and reconstruct just one isolated architectural element of it, it would become a meaningless fragment, for it would no longer be an organic part of the whole, and thus would not serve the initial purpose of preserving the old. Thus, what I tried to do was to treat the reconstructed part as an environmental element that has to be naturally integrated with the newly designed building, to form one coherent functional-visual entity.

The intention was to design the new center as an integral part of the square.

The key question I asked myself was, what is the right thing to do in order to preserve and enhance the spirit of what still exists around there, which is so human and right. Standing in the square I adopted none of the classical approaches. I aimed neither to reconstruct the past nor to dissociate myself from it by enforcing a completely new order. I was looking for a language that *at that point in time* in Bialik Square would create a *meaningful dialogue* between a new, contemporary building and the historical environment.

*Main elevation towards the square.*

*reconstructed part*

## The interrelation between the building and the square

The powerful presence of the building in the square emanates from its being an integral part of it, and not from the efforts to distinguish it from its environment.

This intimate and organic integration was created by several basic means:

*The dimensions of the building* are in harmony with the human scale of the square.

*The façade of the building* defines the boundaries of the square, and therefore determines the feeling it inspires. The orange paint of the building's façade, apparently expected to disturb the tranquility of the square, was the element that complemented the blue color of the sky and the green color of the trees, to create a harmony that inspired peace and serenity in the square. The cornices that jut out at the façade belong morphologically both to the building and to the space next to it, uniting them together. The dialogue between the building and the square continues through the high windows behind which all the indoor "public" areas are located, as well as from the roof terrace overlooking the square.

*The crown on top of the building* provides a graduated *link* to the sky. Its shape was derived from the same language that determined the pattern of the cement tiles of the porch and the relieves on the railing wall. At the front, where the building touches the square, an *entrance porch* was designed for the orchestra to play to the audience sitting in the square, thus creating a physical and human connection between the building and the square.

*The forms of the crown (above), the railing wall relieves (left) and the cement tile (below) are all echoes of one pattern.*

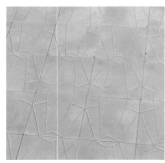

מרכז למוסיקה וספריה
ע"ש פליציה בלומנטל
FELICJA BLUMENTAL
MUSIC CENTER & LIBRARY

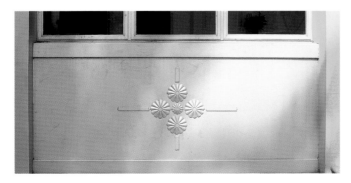

*The left wing
of the building
is made of sil-
ver-painted iron
panels.*

# The interior of the building

Past the main lobby, at the entrance to the building, is the auditorium, separated from it by a glass wall, through which the back garden at the far end can be seen.

At the side of the lobby there is a wide-open staircase, which is an identified beautiful space by itself. It leads to the upper floors, providing a view of all the floors open to it. The high windows alongside the staircase allow daylight into all the parts of the building. The iron balustrades of the stairs and of the auditorium is painted gold, providing a melody of its own. When the sunrays hit these decorated iron balustrades they create beautiful silhouettes on the various surfaces.

The first floor houses the lending library with the catalogues and librarian counter at the entrance. The rear areas are reserved for the notes, scores and books, with access to staff only.

The second floor accommodates the museum of musical instruments and contemporary exhibitions related to music. Further along, past glass partitions are a study and periodicals room and an archive. These three spaces make one visual continuum while preserving the identity and uniqueness of each space.

The top floor houses the audiovisual library that lends discs, videotapes, and records. Further along, beyond the glass partition, is an audiovisual room with a view of the sea.

Extending from this floor, overlooking the square, is a roof terrace that has also a view of the sea.

The details of the building, all designed by me, were not perceived as isolated "designed" fragments, but as part of *one hierarchical language* in which the square, the building and the interior were regarded as *one continuous system*. Each specific detail is derived from the larger whole to which it belongs, which it seeks to enhance, and for whose existence it was responsible. That included the design of the furniture, the lighting fixtures and the choice of color of the flowers in the garden. The form, color and material of each part of the building flow from the *functional* need it serves. Function in this case is conceived as a broad concept, semantically connected to both the *physical and spiritual* comfort experienced by the users in the building.

This concept is manifested, for example, in the following design details:

*The wall between the lobby and the auditorium,* which normally would be solid, is a glass wall that allows a view of the depth of the building immediately upon entrance.

*The six steel columns* that rise to the top of the building are structural, but at the same time their exact location helps to define and distinguish the public areas of each floor.

*The capital of the column,* a functional entity that both separates it from the beam and connects it to it, is distinguished from other parts of the column by its leaf-like shape and its gold color.

*The textured gold color of the walls* in the public areas is different from the color of other spaces.

*The seams* between the stone tiles and the carpets are made of cherry wood, a third material that both joins and separates the two.

The soft reflection of the light when it touches the gold, silver and reddish colors in the space creates a unique feeling that envelops all parts of the building.

Site and ground-floor plan.
1 auditorium
4 entrance porch
5 lobby
6 open staircase
7 café

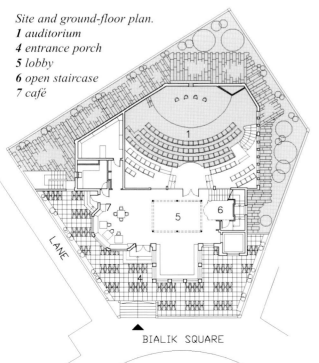

LANE

BIALIK SQUARE

The exact location
of the six columns
helps define the
public area on
each floor.

45

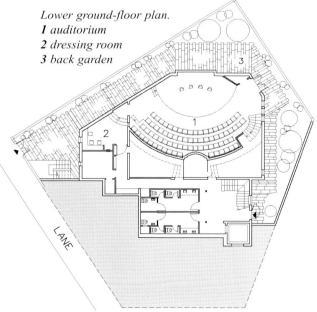

Lower ground-floor plan.
**1** auditorium
**2** dressing room
**3** back garden

*The similarity in form between the ceiling, the glass wall, the gallery and the chairs stems from the common whole to which they belong.*

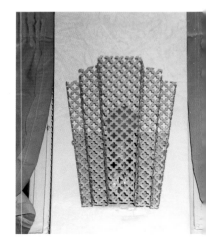

*The textured gold color of the walls in the public areas distinguishes them from the other spaces.*

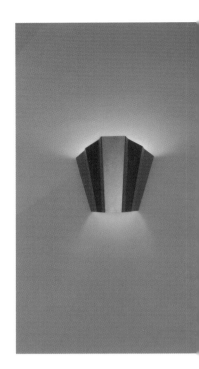

*Catalogues area,
overlooking the
square.*

*First-floor plan –
music lending
library.*
**8** *catalogues and
librarian counter*
**9** *notes, scores,
books*
**10** *administration*
**11** *librarian's
room*

*The iron balustrades provide a melody, enhancing the feeling of the staircase.*

*Second-floor plan.*
**12** *music museum*
**13** *study and periodicals room*
**14** *archive*
**15** *curator's room*

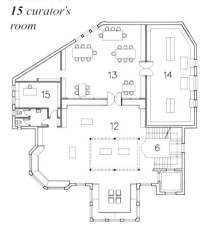

*Study and periodicals room, visually connected to the museum area.*

*The furniture is derived from the larger whole which it seeks to enhance.*

*The square, the building and the back garden form one continuous whole.*

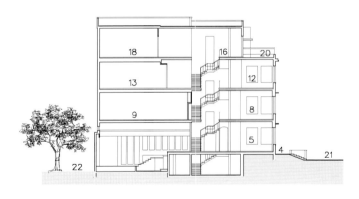

Third-floor plan.
**16** catalogues
and librarian
counter
**17** audiovisual
room
**18** discs, video-
tapes
**19** librarian's
room
**20** roof
terrace

All parts of the
audiovisual
library are visu-
ally connected,
with a view of
the roof terrace
and the sea at
the far distance.

*Grapes stained at the edge of the upper window create a boundary that both connects and separates the glass and the wooden frame.*

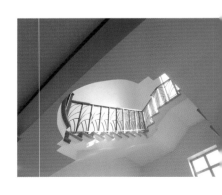

הַבָּנוי לִכְלֵל נְבִנָּה.
חַדֵר צִיּוּן, אֲרְכִיבִים

# Ohel Shem community and school library

**Ohel Shem High School, Ramat Gan, Israel**
**Completion date: 1996**

At the opening ceremony of the library the mayor said: "This library, one of the most dignified in the country, will be a cornerstone and a contribution to the education and preparation of the young generation for the future. It will teach the young that spiritual and moral values are of essence and should be their guiding light."

It seemed to me that beyond its value as a resource center, the creation of an aesthetic learning environment that can be experienced by the students in the library will be an *educational and cultural* value in itself. It will prepare them to regard aesthetics and awareness to the quality of the built environment as guiding values in their life. The spiritual experience and the pleasant ambience I wanted to create for the reader was deeply rooted in the physical structure and the spatial order of the building.

The building itself was situated between two rows of old ficus trees, which dictated the building's overall plan.

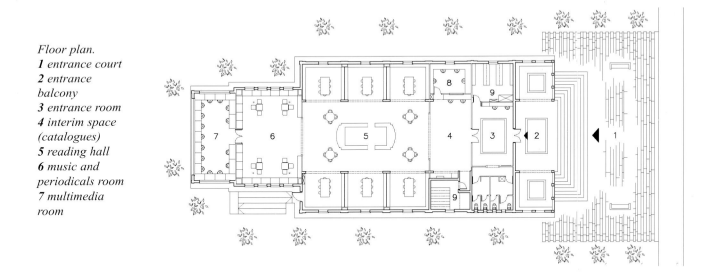

*Floor plan.*
*1 entrance court*
*2 entrance balcony*
*3 entrance room*
*4 interim space (catalogues)*
*5 reading hall*
*6 music and periodicals room*
*7 multimedia room*

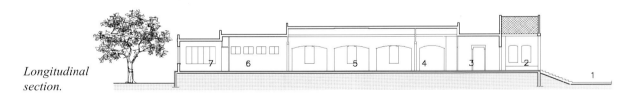

*Longitudinal section.*

*Sequence of
spaces, visually
connected.*

A wide entrance stairway leads to the entrance balcony, where students can "hang out" if they choose. The shaded balcony and the stairway serve as a transition area, which both connects and separates the building and the school's main walkway.

The color chosen for the exterior walls was the hue of the golden leaves that fall outside the building in the autumn, a process which is illustrated in detail in the first chapter of the book. Yellow pigments were mixed with the plaster, creating a perfect harmony with the greenness of the trees and the blue sky.

*View of the main entrance. The court is a transition area between the library and the school's main walkway.*

*Elevation of the main entrance towards the school's main walkway.*

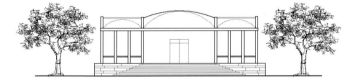

*The stairs and the balcony serve as a transition area between the outdoors and the library.*

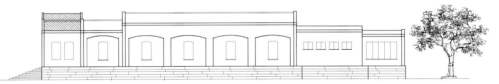

*Side elevation towards the street.*

The interior of the building consists of a sequence of spaces that lead one into another; all visually connected. The entrance hall is a transition area, designated to slow the pace and lower the voice of those entering the library, providing space for the lockers.

The entrance room opens to an open space forming a transition area leading to the reading hall. In here are the catalogues, the copy machines and the display alcove for the new books.

The librarian's counter is placed at a central position in the main reading room. That area is clearly marked by a seven-meter-high arched ceiling. The reading areas at both sides of the main room are built as alcoves that are openly related to the central space, each one dedicated to a specific subject.

In contrast to contemporary libraries, where there is a clear separation between the sitting area and the bookshelves, here the bookshelves embrace the readers, forming an intimate relationship between the reader and the books. Each window at the center of the reading alcoves was aligned with the position of the trees.

*The hand-made printed tiles define the boundaries that both seperate and connect the tiles and the wall.*

*Cross section through the reading hall.*

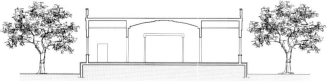

*Transition area
at the entrance
to the reading
room.*

All the interior walls and ceilings are coated with a marble-textured Venetian stucco, creating an ambience of warm yellow on the walls and of pure white on the ceilings.

The design of the furniture, the light fixtures and the choice of colors all constituted an integral part of the design process, and contributed to the pleasant and unique atmosphere experienced by the readers.

The reading room opens to the music and periodicals section. Here the students can lean back in soft armchairs, read magazines or listen to music by earphones. At the far end, entered through glazed doors, is the computer and multimedia room. The different heights of the ceilings in the various rooms create diverse atmospheres directly related to the range of activities.

*Computer and multimedia room.*

*Entrance room.*

*Audiovisual library, music and periodicals section.*

*Each space of activity is distinguished by its own roof.*

*Each reading alcove is distinguished also from the outside.*

*Each reading alcove has a window, aligned with the position of the trees outside.*

# Music library

**Beit Ariela Central City Library, Tel Aviv, Israel**
**Completion date: 1991**

The music library was designed as part of the Tel Aviv central municipal library. The library lends compact discs and videocassettes and offers services. Its level of operations corresponded at the time of completion to that of the most advanced music libraries in the world, and it was the first music library to be built within a public library in Israel.

The entrance to the music library is from the main library. The area allocated for the library is divided into three parts. The furniture used for displaying and storing the music material serves as partitions, forming the separate rooms within the overall space. An entrance room features the librarian's lending counter and a display of videocassettes. An arched opening, forming a gate, leads to the central reading room,

where compact discs are on display. A long table for the readers is placed at the center of the room. At the sides, overlooking the reading area there is an open gallery furnished with bookshelves. Glass doors lead from the central room to an audiovisual room, where individual stations are installed for listening to music and viewing videocassettes. These stations are operated through a central control counter at the front desk.

The furniture is made of cherry wood, the metal railings and stairs leading to the gallery are painted gold, and the carpet is of a warm peach color.

The harmonious relationship between the interior details, the natural materials and the warm colors in the library generates a feeling of elegance and tranquility.

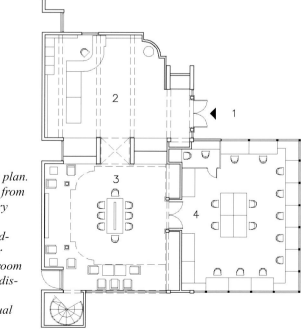

*Main-floor plan.*
*1 entrance from main library*
*2 entrance room – lending counter*
*3 reading room and music display*
*4 audiovisual room*

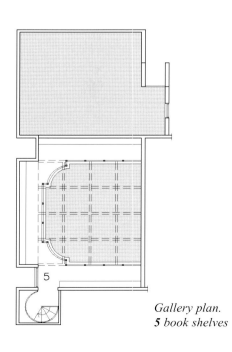

*Gallery plan.*
*5 book shelves*

*View from entrance room to the central room.*

*Entrance door from the main library. Musical instruments are stained on the glass.*

*View from the central room to lending counter at entrance room. The furniture is made of cherry wood.*

*The central room opens to the audiovisual room.*

*The audiovisual room.*

*View to book gallery overlooking the central reading and display room (right).*

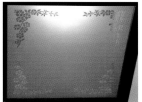

The ceiling is
made of stained-
glass panels.

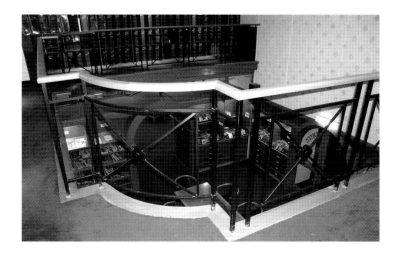

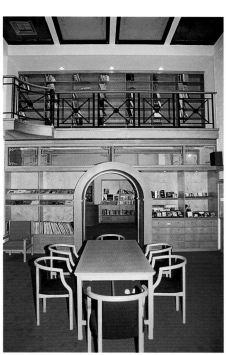

# Central city library and resource center

**Haifa, Israel**
**Competition entry: 1999**

The library is located on Mount Carmel and grows out of the mountain's unique scenery. The experience produced by the library's indoor spaces and outdoor areas will induce a sense of drama and calmness at the same time.

In addition to its role as a cultural and educational center, this library will also serve as a social focal point for the population of Haifa and its surroundings, a place to read a newspaper or meet a friend on the café terrace facing the sea. It will also serve as an information center, providing information on current events in town, job opportunities and leisure activities.

The pedestrian access route from the street to the square is via an open ramp. On entering the site the visitor will first encounter the natural flora (oak trees, carob trees, medicinal plants and silvery boulders) on the site as well as the view of the port and the sea in the north, and that of the Lower Galilee mountains in the east.

Along the hillside there is a covered trellised promenade with benches overlooking the surrounding landscape. At the far edge of the square there is an open amphitheater, facing the mountains, for outdoor performances.

The building was not conceived as a monument imbued with symbolism; its role is to elicit in the visitor a spiritual experience, produced by the simplicity and the elegance of the place.

*The compound
mirrors the har-
mony between
the library build-
ings and its out-
doors, where one
can experience
the natural sur-
rounding land-
scape.*

The entrance hall of the library is built as an atrium. It has an open view of all the library's sections located on ground and first floor levels. Each activity area within the 15,000 square meters of the library has a clear structural definition, affording the user easy orientation within the library.

An elegant stairway connects the entrance hall to the reading rooms area on the first floor. In here is where the visitors can sense through a glass wall the continuity created between the library's indoor space, the square and the view of the sea and mountains, at the distance.

*Site and ground-floor plan.*
*a entrance plaza*
*b promenade*
*c shops and garden café*
*d main entrance to library*
*1 entrance hall*
*2 café and magazines corner*
*3 graphotèque*
*4 childern's library*
*5 newspapers and archive*
*6 music library*
*7 terrace café*

*Lower ground-
floor plan.*
**12** *videothèque*
**13** *archive*
**14** *administration*

Although a contemporary library must be based upon the most advanced technological infrastructure, I believe it still should place the *reader* at the center of attention. It must continue to play its traditional role of providing the reader with a pleasant and friendly environment, similar to the ambience of traditional libraries like the Bibliothèque Sainte-Geneviève in Paris, the Lincoln's Inn Library in London, and others. Unlike most libraries, here there is no separation between the location of the readers' tables and that of the book-shelves in the reading rooms. The books constitute an outer layer that embraces the reader.

*First-floor plan.*
**8** *reading room*
**9** *lending library*
**10** *periodicals*
**11** *classrooms*

*North-east elevation overlooking the sea.*

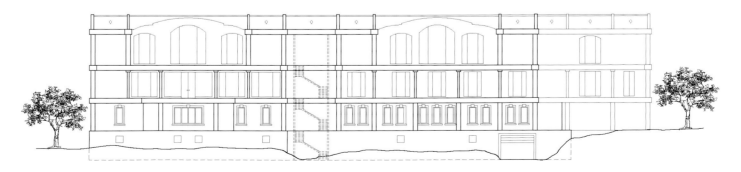

*The reading room overlooking the sea, provides a friendly environment for the reader.*

# Ir Yamim community center

**Natanya, Israel**
**Design phase: 2004**

Natanya, a city located on the coast, is a tourist resort. Ir Yamim, a neighborhood at the southern part of Natanya, is currently undergoing intensive residential, tourist and commercial development. It is populated by immigrants of various origins. This center will accommodate the needs of all south Natanya residents and serve as a valuable means to unite the various ethnic groups.

The site is located on a magnificent sand dune bordering a nature reserve overlooking the sea. An urban square was planned at the front of the building, connecting the building's main entrance with the main road at the edge of the plot. The view of the sea and the nature reserve dictated the unique angle at which the building was placed in relationship to the landscape.

The movement inside the building progresses along an "internal street", where the various activities take place. The "street" lies parallel to the scenery line and opens onto it from the moment the visitor enters the building and along his way.

In front of the back façade of the building, which overlooks the vista, there is a promenade that opens up to an open amphitheater spread out over the downward slope, reminding us of the Roman amphitheater in the neighboring city of Caesarea. The building and the site development will be constructed of regionally quarried yellow sandstone incorporating whitewashed plaster. This beautiful stone, which will give the building and

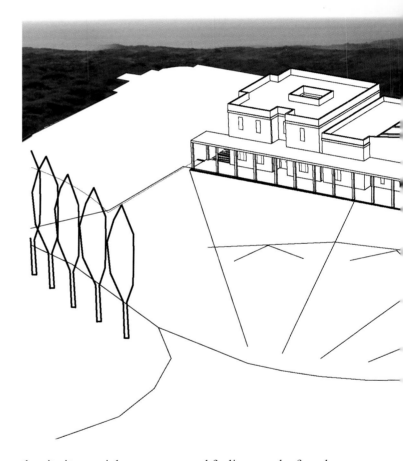

the site its special appearance and feeling, can be found in all ancient coast cities in Israel, including Jaffa, Acre and Caesarea.

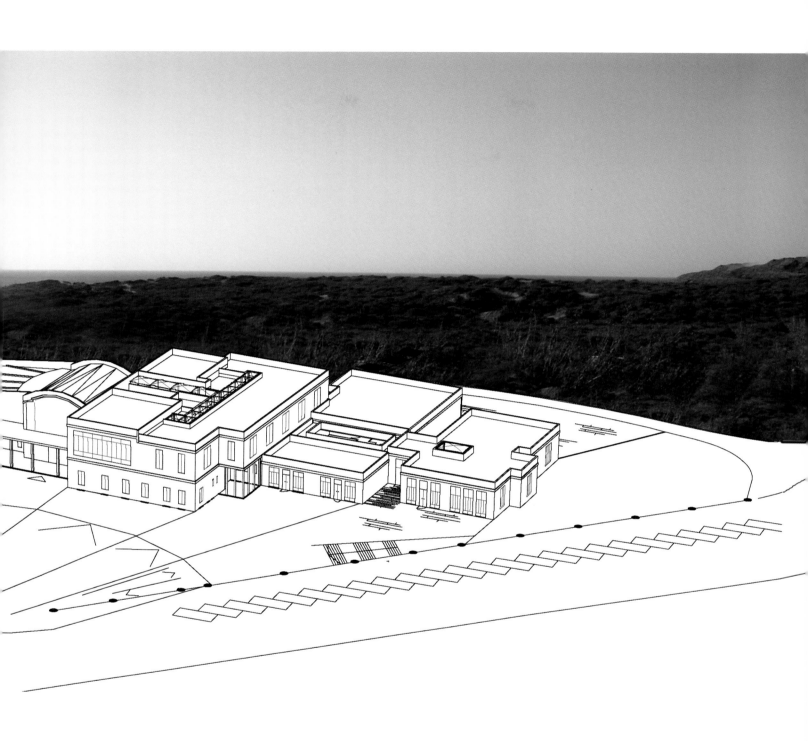

*Perspective view
from the urban
plazza to the
nature reserve.*

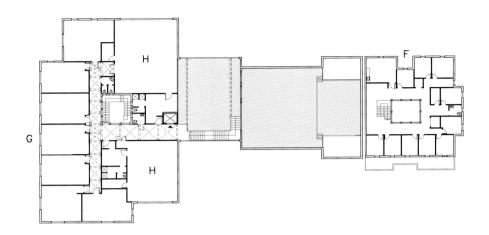

*First-floor plan.*
**g** *activity rooms*
**h** *dance studios*

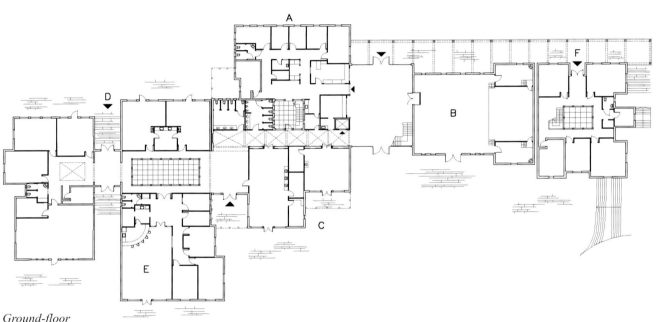

*Ground-floor
plan.*
**a** *administration*
**b** *multipurpose
hall*
**c** *arts studios*
**d** *early childhood
wing*
**e** *youth center*
**f** *music con-
servatory*

*Site and ground-
floor plan.
The view of the
sea and the
nature reserve
dictated the
exact angle and
location of the
different indoor
spaces and
openings.*

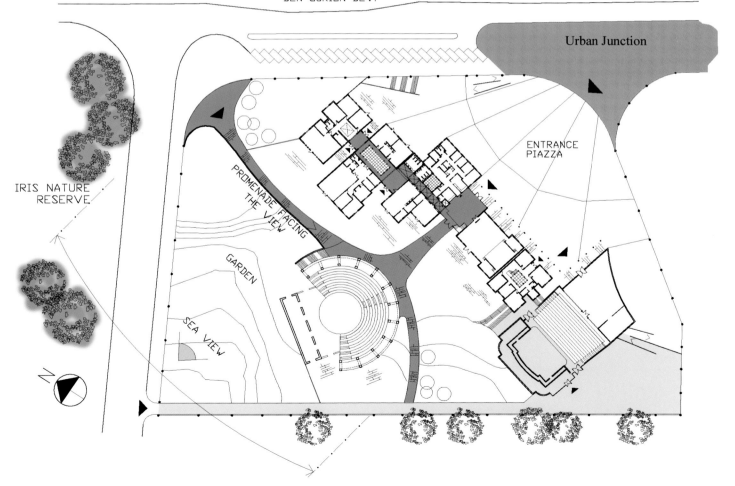

BEN-GURION BLV.

Urban Junction

ENTRANCE
PIAZZA

IRIS NATURE
RESERVE

PROMENADE FACING
THE VIEW

GARDEN

SEA VIEW

N

# The Maimonides Central Sephardic Synagogue

Hadera, Israel
Competition entry: 1988 – first prize
Design phase: 1988

The idea behind the design of the central Sephardic synagogue was to attempt to revive traditional design patterns based on both Maimonides' halakic rulings (the laws he set down in his book *Hayad Hahazaka*) and Talmudic literature as it was passed on to me by the beadles of the synagogues in Safad, capital of the Galilee, home and birthplace of Judaism's mystical stream of the *Kabala*, and infuse into them a new meaning, in line with the program for this synagogue, and in accordance with the immediate landscape.

I endeavored to captivate in this building the timeless spiritual exaltation that we experience in places of worship of every religion, in any culture we know, a feeling that worshippers underwent in synagogues where Maimonides prayed, such as the Iben Denan Synagogue in Fez, Morocco, the Ben-Ezra Synagogue in Cairo, or the Abuhab Sephardic Synagogue in Safad, Israel. That deep feeling that opens your heart when entering places of worship, stems from the structural properties of the building itself.

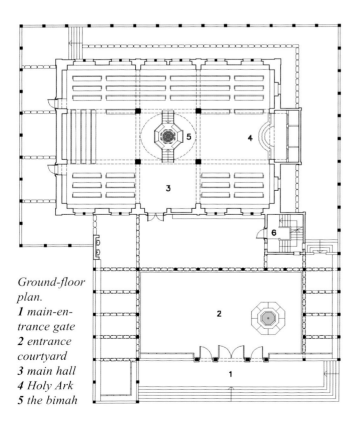

*Ground-floor plan.*
*1 main-entrance gate*
*2 entrance courtyard*
*3 main hall*
*4 Holy Ark*
*5 the bimah*

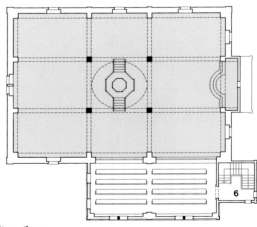

*First-floor plan – women's wing.*
*6 stairs leading to women's wing*

*Cut-away axono-
metric view of the
building.*

81

The courtyard at the front of the building forms a transition area, separating that which is holy from the secular. Access to the courtyard is via a *wide staircase*, located in-between two existing eucalyptus trees "to exalt the house of the Lord". *The gates* at the entrance to the courtyard are the "Gates of Prayer". At the courtyard's center of gravity is a water fountain; water being the symbol of life in all religions.

At the main-entrance door to the building there is a *stair leading down* into the synagogue, as it says, "From the depths I call to thee, Oh Lord."

Main-entrance door.

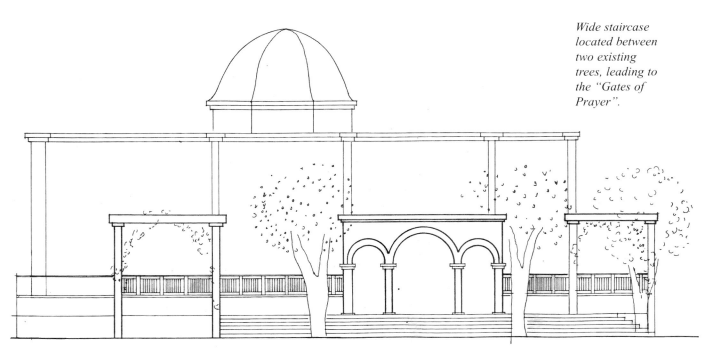

*Wide staircase located between two existing trees, leading to the "Gates of Prayer".*

*Perspective view of the entrance courtyard separating the holy from the secular.*

*Entrance courtyard, Haari Ashkenazic Synagogue, Safad.*

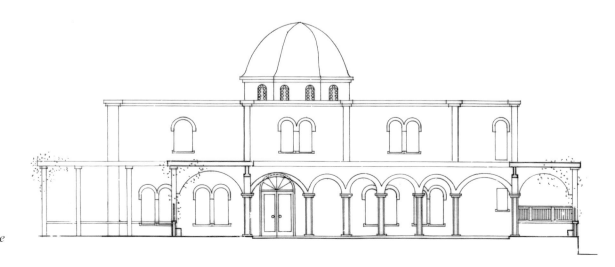

*Main-entrance elevation.*

The synagogue seats 450 worshippers, 300 men in the main hall and 150 in the women's section. The wall of the *Holy Ark* (which holds the Torah scrolls) faces Jerusalem. In the center of the hall there are four pillars, corresponding to the number of the "Matriarchs", structurally dividing the hall into nine sections, corresponding to the nine months of pregnancy.

The Sephardic synagogue had its roots in the Eastern culture of the Islamic lands and thus was influenced by the structure of the mosque. *The seats* (as in mosques) are arranged around the walls, perpendicular to and at an equal distance from the axis that links the Holy Ark and the "bimah" (dais), where the reader of the Torah portion stands.

*Cut-away detail of the dome.*

*The "bimah"* stands on eight pillars, equal to the eight days of Hanukah. Over the "bimah" there is a dome with *twelve windows*, representing the Twelve Tribes. The building is constructed of white plaster incorporated with regionally quarried sandstone used for the frames of the doors and windows, the arches of the arcade and the floor tiles of the courtyard.

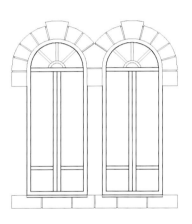

*Construction detail: two windows, forming one window alcove.*

*Traditional patterns of seats along the walls. Yosef Karo Synagogue.*

*"Bimah" with 8 pillars and dome with 12 windows. Abuhav Synagogue, Safad.*

*Perspective
drawing of
the interior.*

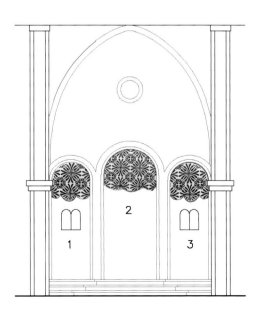

*The Holy Ark
has three doors,
each opened
once a year.*

# Memorial Site for the Fallen Intelligence Servicemen

**Glilot, Tel Aviv, Israel**
**Competition entry: 1982 – purchase prize**

The memorial in honor of the fallen members of the Israeli Intelligence Corps included:

1. An outdoor assembly area for 1000 people, for holding memorial and community services.

2. A memorial corner featuring the names of the fallen.

3. Outdoor assembly sites for the parents and the trainees (soldiers) of the corps' school.

4. A building with a conference room, study rooms and offices.

It was my belief that a peaceful and harmonious *memorial site*, rather than a forceful commemorative statue, which is commonly erected in such cases, will be the appropriate environment for the families of the intelligence community to feel in communion with their loved ones.

The proposed planning process was *fundamentally* different from common planning processes. The members of the community were invited to take an *active* role in the planning of the site. The plan of the site was based on a dynamic set of rules (pattern language), directly responding to the specific needs defined by the intelligence community. This set of rules was to guide the *members of the community* at any stage of the future development of the site. Thus my proposal at the competition stage was more of a *simulation* than a final plan, indicating the possible outcome if this set of rules was to be implemented with the participation of the community members themselves.

Each planning decision taken step by step *on the site* (as illustrated in detail in the first chapter of the book) was marked physically on the ground by stakes and lime, thus enabling the community to easily visualize the plan, and take an active role in its creation. The process of finding the right location for each function was governed by the qualities and

*Perspective drawing of the main path.*

requirements of that specific function. For example, the Memorial Corner featuring the names of the fallen soldiers was located at the far edge of the site, inside the grove, which is the most intimate spot on the site. Here the families can have maximum privacy in their communion with their loved ones.

The final "layout" that emerged on the site was measured and recorded by a surveyor, forming the actual simulation plan.

The plan, developed gradually on the site, was in fact a structure of balance between the patterns and the living reality on the site.

*Perspective
drawing of the
outdoor assem-
bly area and
main building.*

*Overall view of
the site from the
main-entrance
gate. Planning
decisions taken
on the site and
marked on the
ground.*

*Perspective drawing of the path leading to the memorial corner.*

*The memorial corner was located at the most intimate spot – at the far end of the site.*

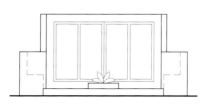

*The wall of names and the two benches at its sides form the memorial corner.*

*Transverse section of site. The interrelations between the building, the main path and the outdoor areas (right).*

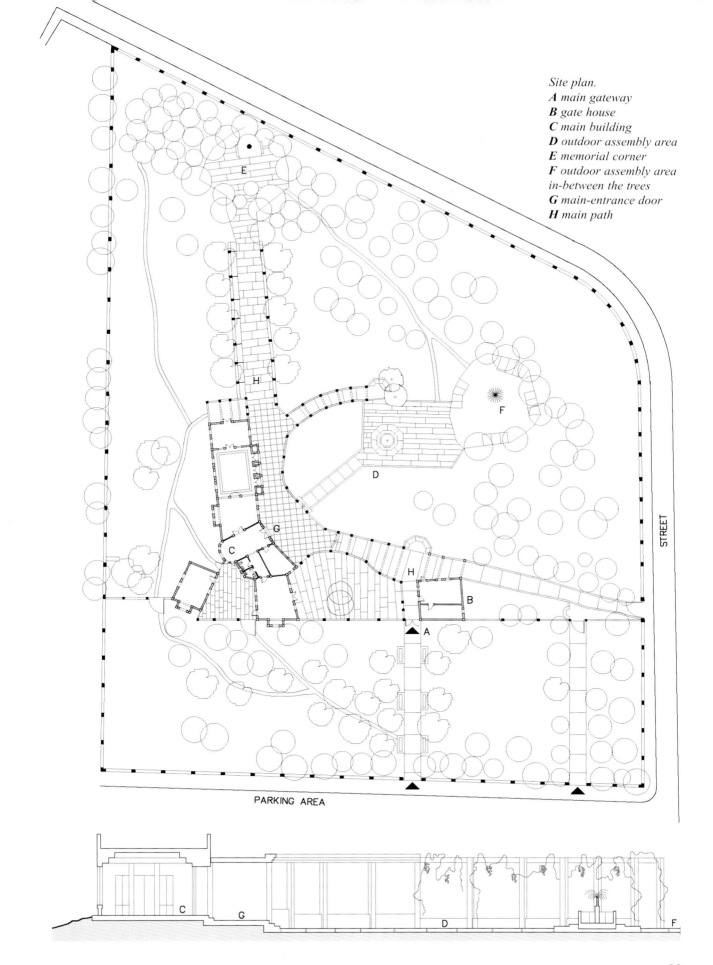

*Site plan.*
*A main gateway*
*B gate house*
*C main building*
*D outdoor assembly area*
*E memorial corner*
*F outdoor assembly area*
*in-between the trees*
*G main-entrance door*
*H main path*

STREET

PARKING AREA

89

# The Israel National War Memorial Center

**Mount Eitan, Jerusalem, Israel**
**Competition entry: 1995**

The Israel National War Memorial Center was to include:

1. A memorial center commemorating all the soldiers fallen in Israel's wars and military campaigns since the beginning of the 20th century.

2. A museum complex presenting the history of the Israel Defense Forces (IDF) and the struggle of Israeli society to survive in the Land of Israel, from the earliest Zionist settlements to the present day.

Wars, warriors and fallen warriors are an inseparable part of the daily existence and reality, personal and collective, in Israel. They play a major role in our lives in this country. In Israel the army is not regarded as a violent force, but rather as "the people's army", representing the individual and the society as a whole. It is an integral part of the cultural creation and value formation of the Israeli society.

Since architecture reflects values, human values can generate humane architecture. Therefore it seems to me that projects related to military matters need not necessarily be forceful. The construction of a national center is in itself an act loaded with symbolism, much more so when it is designed to commemorate the human and personal facet of the warrior. In my mind, such a humane message cannot be conveyed through an architectural monument using various conceptual images, but rather through a direct emotional experience created by the linkage between man and place. I believe that the architectural order I proposed has the power to do so. The particular design proposal for the site was tightly linked to the spiritual, cultural and physical forces of Mount Eitan. Mount Eitan is a holistic entity in the landscape, with a strong sense of "a place". The structured order I designed for the site does not interfere with the visitor's perception of the natural characters of the site, but grows out of it.

*The holiness of the landscape symbolizes a timeless environmental order and was the starting point for determining the character of the site.*

The 40,000 square meters were planned not as a single monolithic building, but as a linear structure, composed of an identified complex of separate buildings, organically integrated in the landscape, each corresponding to a particular function as dictated by the program.

The site's focal points are:

a. The *Path of Names* which runs in the form of a wall along the periphery of the site, is visible from every point on the site. Every fallen soldier has an individual corner along the path, where his name is carved. The wall blends gently with the landscape, a gentleness that expresses the humanity of the fallen soldiers.

The *Path of Names* marks the border of the site. It is an end and a beginning. On the one hand, as a wall it protects the values exhibited in the museum, the heart of the site, on the other hand it faces the open space, where one can see settlements, for the freedom and protection of which these soldiers have fought and fallen.

Where the *Path of Names* interacts with the lanes coming from the pavilions exhibiting Israel's battles, movement slows down. Here there are sitting corners, facing the scenery, for here time stands still.

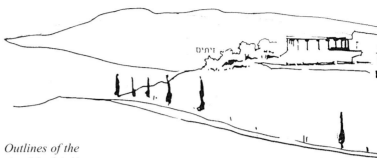

*Outlines of the site (black ink) The site's presence evolves from the appearance of its boundaries. The path of names is the boundary where something ends but at the same time something new begins.*

*Site plan.*
*1 college and hostel*
*2 visitors center*
*3 peace square: well and olive grove*
*4 war pavilions*
*5 amphitheater*
*6 the Path of Names*
*7 stately entrance to the site*
*8 memorial open space at the entrance to the site*
*9 entrance gate*
*10 the Lane of Time; museum complex*
*11 war pavilion open terrace*

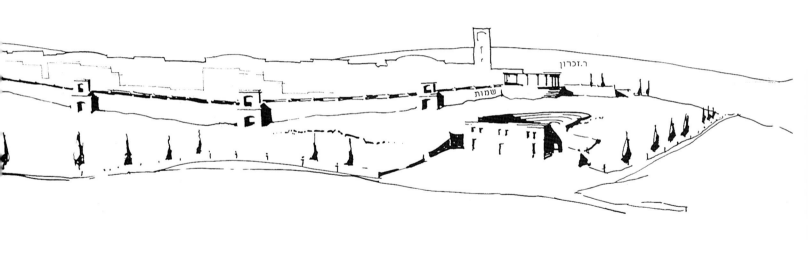

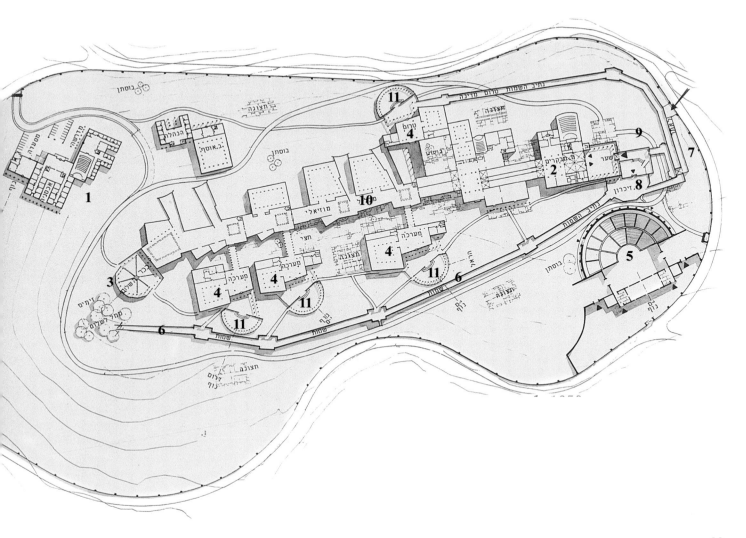

b. The *Lane of Time* forms the backbone of the site, along which are situated the galleries exhibiting IDF values, and from which fork the pavilions exhibiting the wars and battles. It nourishes on the legacy of the waves of immigrants who have been coming here since the early 20th century and whose story is exhibited in the pavilions along the lane. They are the central force that formed and generated the *Lane of Time,* much like the *Panathenaic way* in ancient Athens that led from the city gate to the Acropolis, where the procession of masses of people gathered along that way became the central force in the creation of the urban development of Athens.

The *Lane of Time* runs from the memorial area at the entrance to the site to the olive grove (the symbol of peace) at its end. That grove symbolically forms an intersection between the water (symbolizing life) coming from the well at the end of the lane and the *Path of Names.*

*Like a main artery that is fed from small veins, the Lane of Time was fed by waves of immigrants who came to this land over the years.*

*Eitan Mountain.*

*People's movement on the site along the axis created between the gates. Points in time in the museum complex and panoramic focuses along the Path of Names.*

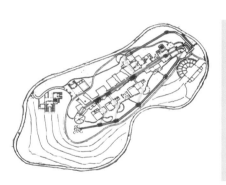

*Ancient Rome, Via Sacra.*

*The way created along the axis between the gates, religious and public buildings and squares.*

*Ancient Athens, the Panathenaic Way.*

*The movement of people from the town gate to the Acropolis was the major driving force in the urban development of Athens.*

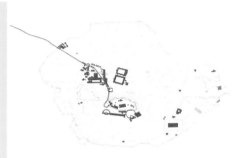

Memorial open
space.

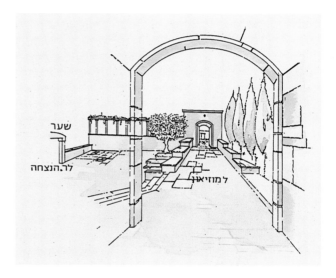

Entrance gate
to the site.

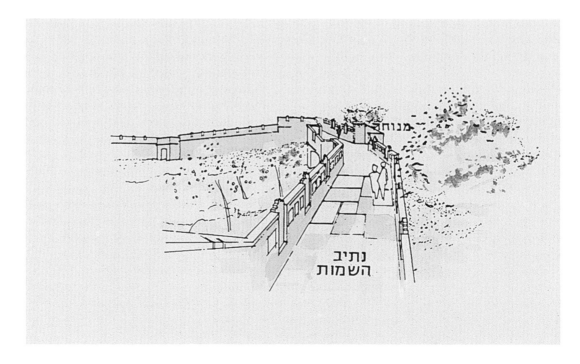

The Path
of Names.

The building materials to be used in the project will blend the traditional with the contemporary. The building stones will be of the kind found at archeological sites and used in monasteries in the area. The water and the orchards will be the link to tradition and to the physical and cultural roots of the land of Israel.

*Jerusalem,*
*Yad Avshalom*
*(1st century*
*AC).The stone*
*used for the*
*building echoes*
*the feeling of*
*this monument.*

*Sandro Botticelli,*
*"Noli Me Tangere".*
*The opening on*
*the right is*
*towards the past,*
*the one on the*
*left is the gate to*
*the future.*

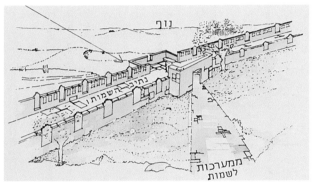

*The Path of*
*Names is the link*
*between the*
*entrance gate to*
*the pavilions of*
*past wars and*
*the panoramic*
*view open to the*
*future.*

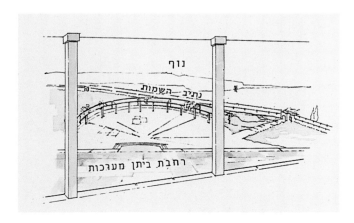

*A view from the*
*war pavilions*
*open space to*
*the Path of*
*Names and the*
*scenery.*

*Perspective sec-*
*tion through site.*

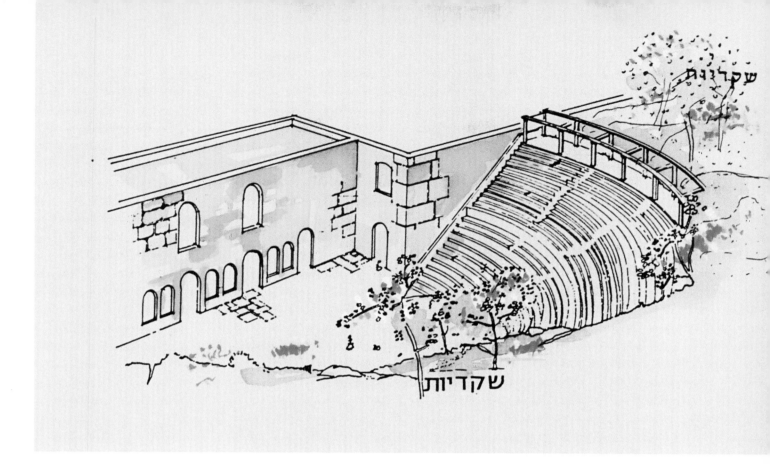

שקדיות

שקרונות

The open
amphitheatre
developed natu-
rally from the
structure of the
site and benefit-
ed from the
scenery of the
almond trees.

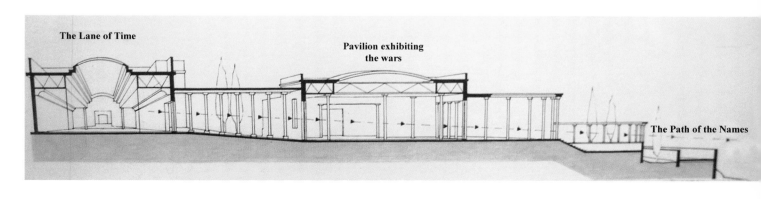

**The Lane of Time**

**Pavilion exhibiting
the wars**

**The Path of the Names**

# Senior-citizens day center

**Tel Aviv, Israel**
**Completion date: 1988**

*The main entrance to the site is reached through an alley from the main road. The entrance gate is located between two eucalyptus trees that form a natural gate.*

The day center for the senior citizens is located at the heart of Tel Aviv, an area of historic value, featuring buildings dated from the 1920s and onwards. These buildings possess calmness and simplicity, qualities and spirit I aspired to preserve in the design of the new center, and thus create an *island of tranquility* within the busy metropolis of Tel Aviv.

The day center was designed to provide social and cultural services as well as occupation for the elderly population in the area. First and foremost I wanted it to inspire the feeling of *home*, not of an institution. Instead of the coldness normally associated with such institutions, I wanted to generate warmth that will encourage the elderly to visit and spend time there.

All the planning decisions regarding the site plan as a whole and each of its buildings were made in a piecemeal process on the site itself. The final plan was an outcome of the interaction between the various patterns chosen for the project and the living reality of the site.

The site plan of the center will be illustrated through the set of patterns, which created its language. (The names of the patterns and the quotations are taken from the book *A Pattern Language.*)

## Main entrance gate

"Place the main entrance of the building at a point where it can be seen immediately from the main avenues ..." The entrance to the site was located between two eucalyptus trees that formed a natural gate.

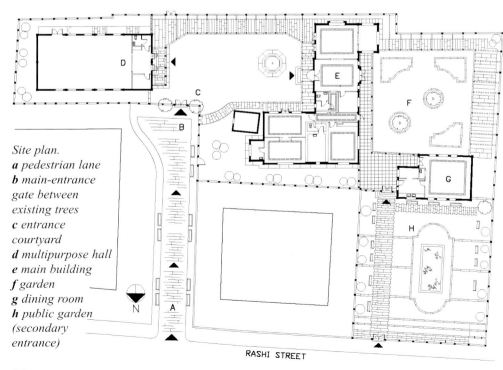

*Site plan.*
*a pedestrian lane*
*b main-entrance gate between existing trees*
*c entrance courtyard*
*d multipurpose hall*
*e main building*
*f garden*
*g dining room*
*h public garden (secondary entrance)*

RASHI STREET

## Site repair

"Buildings must always be built on those parts of the land which are in the worst condition, not the best ..." The most beautiful areas were left open.

*Model of the center.*

## Building complex

"Never build large monolithic buildings. Whenever possible translate your building program into a building complex, whose parts manifest the actual social facts of the situation ..." The building took a form of a collection of wings; connected by arcades and trellised walks.

## Wings of light

"Buildings which displace natural light as the major source of illumination are not fit places to spend the day ..." The building complex was arranged so that it broke into wings as long and narrow as we could design them, allowing the natural light to penetrate into all the floor areas.

*Sun in the dining room (left) and in the living room (right).*

## South (sun) facing outdoor

"People use open spaces if it is sunny and do not use it if it isn't ..." The wings of the buildings were placed to the north and west of the outdoor spaces, keeping the outdoor spaces to the east and south, thus allowing both the outdoor and the indoor spaces to benefit from the sun.

*A large entrance
courtyard behind
the gate forms a
graceful passage
from the street
to the building
complex.*

*The terrace at
the secondary
entrance forms a
transition area
between the pub-
lic garden and
the building
complex.*

# Entrance transition

"Buildings with a graceful transition between the street
and the inside are more tranquil than those which open
directly off the street ..." The entrance courtyard at the
main entrance and the roofed terrace at the secondary
entrance both act as transition areas.

*The sense of
enclosure is
generated by
the well-defined
boundaries,
formed by the
buildings'
façades on the
one side and the
pergolas with
the benches on
the other.*

## Positive outdoor space

"Outdoor spaces which are merely 'left over' between
buildings will, in general, not be used ..." The outdoor
spaces which lie in-between the buildings were
positively defined by the wings of the buildings, the
arcades and the trellised walks around them. The
outdoor spaces are entities, with a positive quality,
carefully designed as an inseparable part of the layout
of the buildings.

*The trellised
walk forms a
boundary that
both connects
and separates
the courtyard
and its adjacent
lots.*

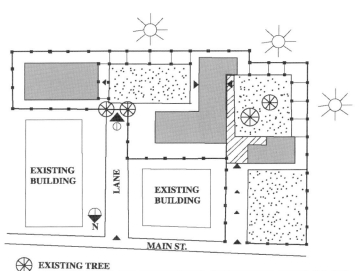

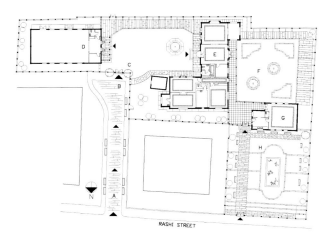

Site-plan scheme. A structure of balance between the patterns chosen for the center and the forces acting on the site. The order within the piecemeal process was governed by the generic structure of the language as a whole.

Site plan.

Floor plan (main building E).
1 entrance hall
2 living room
3 library
4 office
5 classroom
6 parlour
7 arts & crafts studio
8 ceramics studio
9 storage

EXISTING TREE

Longitudinal section.

Elevation with main entrance to the courtyard.

Elevation of the building and the arcade leading to back garden.

## A lively courtyard

The feeling of vivacity in the courtyard emanates from the pathways crossing it as well as from the lively dialogue with the indoor activities, made possible by the doors and windows that open onto it, as well as with the people sitting on the benches along the trellised walks. The center of energy that emerged and became the heartbeat of the courtyard was an outcome of that which surrounded it. Thus the location of the fountain, which was determined only after the completion of the courtyard and the buildings around it, was a mere definition of what "was there" all along.

*Main-entrance courtyard.*

*Stepping in from the main entrance door, a view of the back garden is offered through the room.*

Since the entrance hall has a unique function, it was given a different architectural treatment, identifiable on entering it. Its roof is distinguished from the other roofs, clearly visible from the entrance courtyard. Its ceiling is convex and high and its floor tiles are white, decorated with black, as against the flat ceiling and yellow tiles of the other rooms.

Glazed doors open onto the back garden, leading to an arcade that gradually connects the main building both to the garden and to the dining room at its side.

The inner garden was built where an old and tall pine tree stands. Its exact boundaries – the location of the arcade, the dining room and the vine trellis walks were drawn by a process of approaching the tree and retreating from it, so as to allow the tree the necessary living space it needed.

The secondary entrance to the center is via the public garden designed to serve both the users of the center and the residents of the neighborhood and the city as a whole.

*The secondary
entrance to the
center via the
public garden.*

*Elevation of sec-
ondary entrance
from the public
garden.*

Each wing serves a different activity, and thus is clearly distinguished by its distinct structural elements, such as a different roof or corner columns protruding from the wall. The colored thresholds and well-defined framed "gates" between the different spaces help to both separate and connect them, while emphasizing the sense of passing from one space to another.

*The "gate" in-between the different rooms gives the sense of passing from one space to another.*

*Different patterns of the same language used for different rooms both identify each room and unite them all together.*

*Different lumi-
naires were
designed for
different rooms.*

112

*A corner of tran-
quility under the
vine trellis.*

The construction details, the interior and the
materials used for the building were regarded as
inseparable components of the design process, all
being inherently responsible for the feeling of
calmness created in the center and for enhancing the
pleasant spirit which existed in the area as a whole
prior to our intervention.

# *Residential and mixed developments*

# Residential neighborhood in a kibbutz
## Structural changes in kibbutz life require a new concept of housing

**Kibbutz Maagan Michael, Israel**
**Completion date: stage 1 2001,**
**stage 2 2005**

## From quantitive uniformity to qualitative equality

The social, economic and physical structure of the collective known as a "kibbutz" was founded in Israel in the early 20th century. Its uppermost value since its very beginning was *equality*, translated in most realms of community life not as equality of opportunities, in its qualitative sense, but rather in its *quantitative* sense, as formal uniformity. This dogmatic equality obliterated the self-identity and uniqueness of the individual and saw him only as part of the collective.

In recent years, however, this old conception of equality has been redefined in many respects. The social structure reverted back to the nuclear family, with children raised at home, and no longer in a communal house where they were regarded as the possession of the community as a whole. Wages, previously based on the notion that every member contributed according to his or her own ability, but was supported according to his or her needs, have now become differential, based on one's contribution.

Housing in the kibbutz is perhaps the last fortress of the old and simplistic conception of equality, a conception that now more than ever can change. According to this conception, houses are regarded as static *models* of *predetermined* uniform shape, arbitrarily positioned on the building site. Environmental factors, such as the direction of light or the angle open to the view on any specific plot, are disregarded, and the result is that all houses have an identical plan, including the same elevations. Thus a tenant whose window *happens* to face the orchard has the advantage on the one whose window faces the cow shed.

This approach created a qualitative inequality between the houses and inequality of opportunities among the tenants. Moreover, the outcome of this dogmatic approach was that houses built in the desert environment of the Negev or the hilly Galilean environment were exactly the same.

The new model I implemented in the design of the new houses in kibbutz Maagan Michael was *fundamentally* different. The planning process I adopted was based on patterns that were common to all the houses, patterns that grew out both of the social structure of the kibbutz and the geographic location facing the sea. When these *common patterns* were used in *different site conditions*, *a variety* of houses emerged, sharing one architectural language.

Kibbutz Maagan is situated on a hill, with the new neighborhood on the western side that faces the sea.

*House type A.*

*House type B.*

## Planning the neighborhood on the site

Each planning decision, from the positioning of the house on the site, through the determination of the direction of its entrance in relation to the path, and unto the location of each window, was taken *on the site of each plot*. The position of each house in relation to the others was determined so as to ensure that each one has an open view of the water and can enjoy the breeze coming from the sea. To determine the level of each house so that one could see the sea while sitting on the terrace, I used a crane to lift me up to where I could see the sea. This height was measured and the level of the house was determined accordingly.

*An open view
to the sea in-
between and
through the
houses.*

*Site plan. The
position of each
house was deter-
mined on the
site, in relation
to the other
houses, so as to
ensure an open
view of the sea.*

SEA VIEW

119

At the center of the neighborhood, a path was planned connecting the promenade that runs along the water and the path that runs from the communal dining hall at the heart of the kibbutz to the neighborhood. What dictated the course of the path was my wish to

*To determine the level of each house so that one could see the sea while sitting on the terrace, I used a crane to lift me up to where I could see the sea.*

see the water from every spot along the path. The houses were arranged in small clusters, sharing a communal open space. Unlike the traditional pattern in the kibbutz, where all open spaces, called "the lawn", are communal and the buildings are dispersed arbitrarily in-between, here the secondary paths running between the houses defined in a non-formal way, with no fences, the "private" zone of each family. This sense of "private territory" unexpectedly created a new reality in which each family started to grow its own garden. This new pattern of behavior could not have developed in the traditional model, where the open spaces in-between the houses were planned as a property used and maintained by everyone, and therefore of no one.

120

At this stage the site plan was completed. The position of each house in the neighborhood in relation to the paths and its position in relation to the sea *produced different types of house plans*. On plots where the entrance from the path was in the same direction as the sea view, type A plan emerged. Here the entrance was through the main garden to the living-dining area that faced the view. On plots where the entrance was from the opposite direction of the sea view, type B plan developed, and the entrance was through the opposite side of the garden and living areas.

In front of each house there is a bicycle rack (the only means of transport allowed within the boundaries of the kibbutz). Next to the entrance door a place for muddy boots was allocated, a symbol of the kibbutz.

The walls are all whitewashed light blue, complemented by regionally quarried sandstone characterizing the construction details.

The introduction of a conceptually new model in a very rigid social framework became possible now, as a result of an overall change in the reality of the kibbutz communities.

*Type A – entrance floor.*

*Type B – entrance floor.*

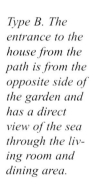

*Type B. The entrance to the house from the path is from the opposite side of the garden and has a direct view of the sea through the living room and dining area.*

122

*Panoramic view. Stages 1 and 2.*

*The windows are the eyes of the building. The window at the dining area is framing the sea view.*

*Type A. The entrance to the house from the path is through the garden. Both are in the direction of the sea view.*

124

*The construction
details stem from
their unique
functional role
within the whole.*

# Hashomer apartments and shops

**Tel Aviv, Israel**
**Completion date: 2004**

*The new building preserves the spirit of the existing historic environment.*

This building is located at the heart of Tel Aviv's historical area, on a side pedestrian street adjacent to the city's central food market. This quarter dates back to the early thirties of the 20th century. In contrast to contemporary apartment buildings, most of which create an anonymous and uniform environment, thus providing not more than a shelter, here an effort was made to design a building with the kind of human and friendly spirit that characterizes this old quarter.

The walk from the street to the building is via a sequence of transition areas that open onto each other and bring the residents home gradually. The entrance to the semi-private garden alongside the building is via a visible red metal gate that opens from the sidewalk. The central part of the façade which is facing the private path is distinguished by the high windows of the staircase. The orange trees planted along the path adorn the building's main-entrance door. The shops at the front of the ground floor open onto the pedestrian street, forming an extension to the arts and crafts fair held there. The back façade features small studio apartments that open onto private gardens.

*Simulation of the building before construction.*

*Ground-floor plan.*
*A, B, C garden apartments*
*1 entrance gate to residential wing*
*2 path leading to entrance lobby*
*3 main-entrance lobby*
*4 shops*
*7 private garden*

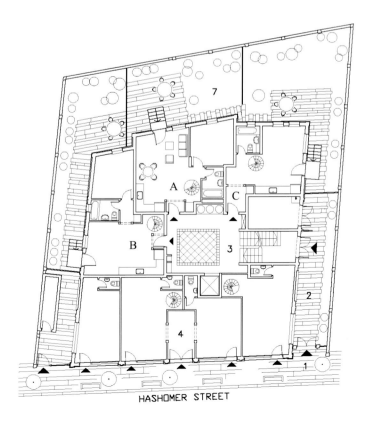

HASHOMER STREET

126

That entrance door leads to a spacious staircase, which opens onto a spacious lobby on each floor of the building. High windows offering a view of the garden illuminate that space.

*High windows offer daylight and a view of the garden.*

The feeling of
the space stems
from the interre-
lations between
the colors, the
materials and
the light.

The spacious
staircase opens
onto the lobby
on all floors.

129

*The finish of the public area walls is of a unique silvery texture.*

The pattern of gradual transition from the public street to the private building, by spaces that both connect and separate them, is repeated inside the apartments. An entrance hall leads gradually from the main-entrance door at the lobby of the apartment to the living areas. Each apartment was designed slightly differently, according to its specific location in the building, so that it interlocks either with the street or the garden next to it.

*Garden apartment (type C). View from the entrance hall to garden exit.*

*Garden apartment (type A). View to entrance hall and stairs leading to basement (right).*

*Garden apartment (type B). View through dining area to garden exit.*

On the higher floors there are one- and two-bedroom apartments. Those at the roof level have roof terraces that offer a magnificent view of the sea of Tel Aviv at the distance.

The balconies and the "French windows" separate the street and the garden from the apartments and at the same time create the ongoing live dialogue between them.

The use of plaster for the exterior, stone for the windowsills and thresholds, the very high windows, and the decorated mosaic used for the floor tiles and stairs, all originated from the architectural language inherent in the place where this building was designed.

*Typical floor plan – one-bed-room apartments.*

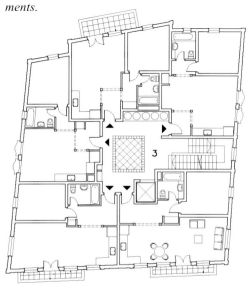

*Gradual transition from entrance hall through living area to the balcony.*

134

*Ongoing dialogue between the building and the street.*

*The particular construction details create the feeling of the whole.*

*The mailboxes. A detail designed as an inseparable part of the overall architectural plan.*

*The balcony
helps to enhance
the ongoing
live dialogue
between the pri-
vate and the
public domain.*

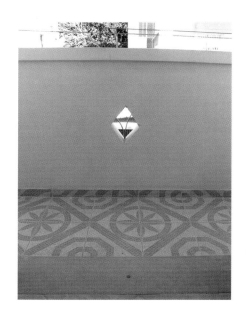

*The golden color of the ground floor distinguishes it from the upper floors. The roof floor is the lightest in color.*

*Roof apartment.
Sequence of
spaces leading
from entrance
hall through liv-
ing area to bed-
room wing.*

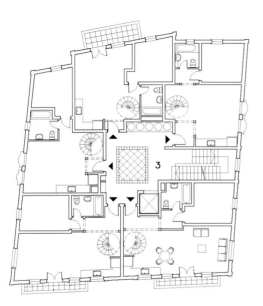

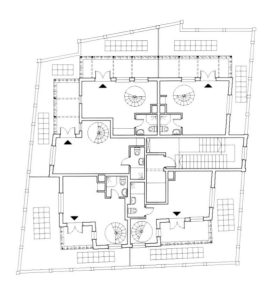

*Third- and
fourth-floor
plan – two-
bedrooms roof
apartments
(leftt).*

*Master bedroom
and roof terrace
on fourth floor
(right).*

*The master bed-
room opens to a
roof terrace that
offers a view of
the sea and of
ancient Jaffa.*

*Roof terrace.*
*The blue tiles*
*mark the*
*boundery of the*
*transition area*
*between the*
*indoors and the*
*terrace.*

# Student dormitories

**Technion Institute of Technology, Haifa, Israel**
**Competition entry: 2001**

The dormitory project was designed to include some 250 apartment units, some studio apartments as well as two-rooms units for roommates or married couples.

The natural scenic values unique to the Carmel Mountain where the site is located, including the panoramic view of the sea, have always been a crucial factor in the development of the city of Haifa. These are values that I aspired to preserve, both in the design of the indoors and in the position of the outdoors.

The site was located on the hill side. The proposal was to provide the students living on the west side of the site, at the bottom of the hill, a convenient pedestrian access to the ring road situated at the top of the site, about 10 meters above, leading to the various faculty buildings. To overcome this tough topography, it was proposed to enable two types of movement: a quick one, via a vertical tower of elevators, and a slow one, via a pedestrian "green path" along a terraced garden. That path stretches along the terraces, from the intersection at the upper level, which leads the students from the dormitory area to the faculty, to the public square at the bottom level.

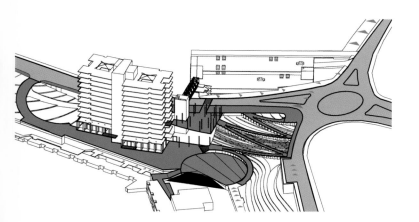

*Slow-movement scheme for pedestrians via a terraced garden.*
■ *for the use of the neighborhood as a whole*

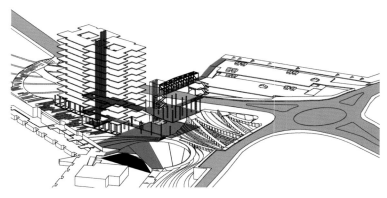

*Fast-movement scheme via a tower of elevators.*
■ *for the use of the neighborhood as a whole*
▥ *for the use of the new dormitories only*

*View of the buildings and terraced garden from the public square at the bottom level of the site.*

Ring Rd

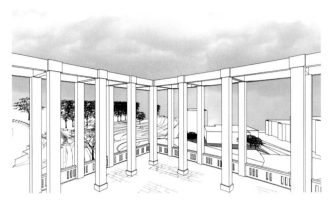
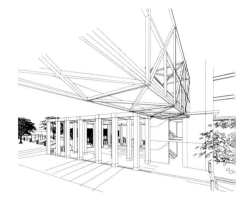

The two pedestrian routes intersect with horizontal links to the upper ring road, the public square at the bottom level of the site and the view terrace adjacent to the upper entrance lobby of the apartment towers.

The view terrace overlooking the public square below creates a visual dialogue between students at both levels.

The site plan was fully adapted to the hill's topographical structure. Despite the high density dictated by the program, maximum areas were allocated for active outdoor spaces. The dormitory mass was divided into two towers, each with its own entrances, both from the upper street level and from the public square.

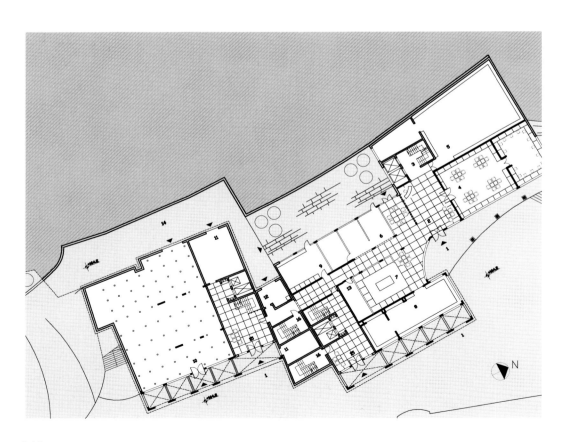

*Entrance-floor plan – dormitories and public areas at the bottom level of the site.*

*Observation terrace at the upper street level overlooking the public square below.*

*Perspective view of the project from the upper street.*

*Entrance-floor plan. Dormitories at the upper street level.*

Access to the inner apartments is via hallways overlooking an atrium flooded with daylight filtering in through the glass dome above. The hallways are interspersed with spacious sitting areas overlooking the dramatic scenery.

The various elements of the building's envelope were designed as an alternating repetition of pre-cast elements. The friendliness emanating from the building façades and dissolving the impression of the mass was produced both by the form of the different elements and by the use of elements mixed with colored pigment alternating with elements of plain concrete.

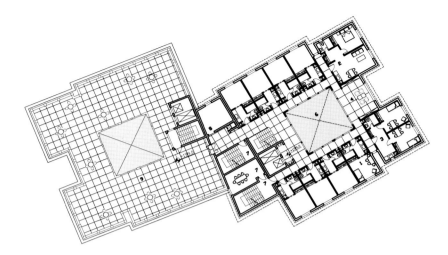

*Roof-floor plan – faculty apartments, public roof terrace overlooking the scenery.*

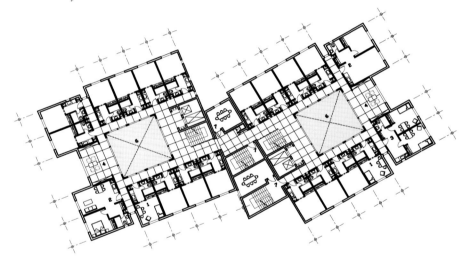

*Typical-floor plan – dormitory apartments.*

*The envelope of the building designed as pre-cast elements.*

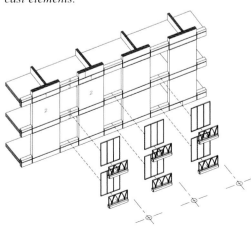

*Spacious public sitting bays overlooking the sea, creating intervals at the passages that lead to the apartments.*

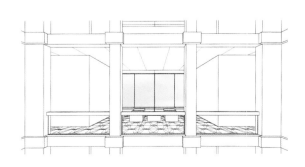

146

*Perspective section through the public square, the terraced garden and the parking.*

*Perspective section through the building and the atrium.*

# "Villas City" residential neighborhood

**Rishon Lezion, Israel**
**Competition entry: 1988 – first prize**

The design competition for the "Villas City" neighborhood on the Rishon Lezion sand dunes required a plan for 900 private houses on plots of 250 to 500 square meters per house. The given site plan dictated the streets network, the boundaries of each lot and the building lines. In addition to the design of each individual house, we were required to design the public spaces in the neighborhood as a whole.

My main objective was to plan a residential environment where people would feel a profound sense of belonging and identification.

The process by which a new residential neighborhood of this kind is normally planned and subsequently developed is a mechanistic one, based on a dogmatic and uniform set of rules, unrelated to the particular reality of the site or the unique family needs. The houses and streets are treated as autonomous fragments, functionally separated. The houses are perceived as static objects, named "models", that are uniform in their predetermined form, superimposed arbitrarily on the site, wherever it happens to be.

In order to avoid the barrenness and alienation that characterize such neighborhoods, my proposal was based on different assumptions:

1. Although families have common interests, each one is unique and its needs differ from those of the others. The concept of an "average home", designated for the "the average person", is a fundamentally destructive one.

2. Houses cannot be conceived as static "models" to be duplicated and copied arbitrarily from one place to another. The structure of the house must grow out of the forces acting on different sites and the specific needs of each family.

3. Although the plots themselves have common characteristics, the smallest differences between them, that stem from their different location in the neighborhood, should be taken into account. A northern plot cannot be treated in the same way as a southern one; a house on a plot that opens onto a main street cannot be planned in the same way as one situated on a plot that opens onto a lane, etc.

4. The house, the street and the neighborhood should be regarded as *one continuous whole*, where each of these elements *is dependent upon the interrelations between them.*

However, the desire to give each house its own identity did not mean we could allow the neighborhood to look like the Tower of Babel, with each house appearing to have been dropped from another planet. There had to be a *common language* shared by all, at all levels of scale, a language that would define the desirable relationships between the street and the houses as well as the common architectural patterns and details of the houses themselves.

The basic types of houses proposed for the neighborhood included duplexes, row houses and single homes. The use of *common patterns* on *different sites with varied environmental conditions* ultimately produced *the distinctiveness and the variety of houses* in different parts of the neighborhood**.** The spatial patterns, the structural details, the colored plaster and the refined sandstone details, which were common to all, united them to one family of houses.

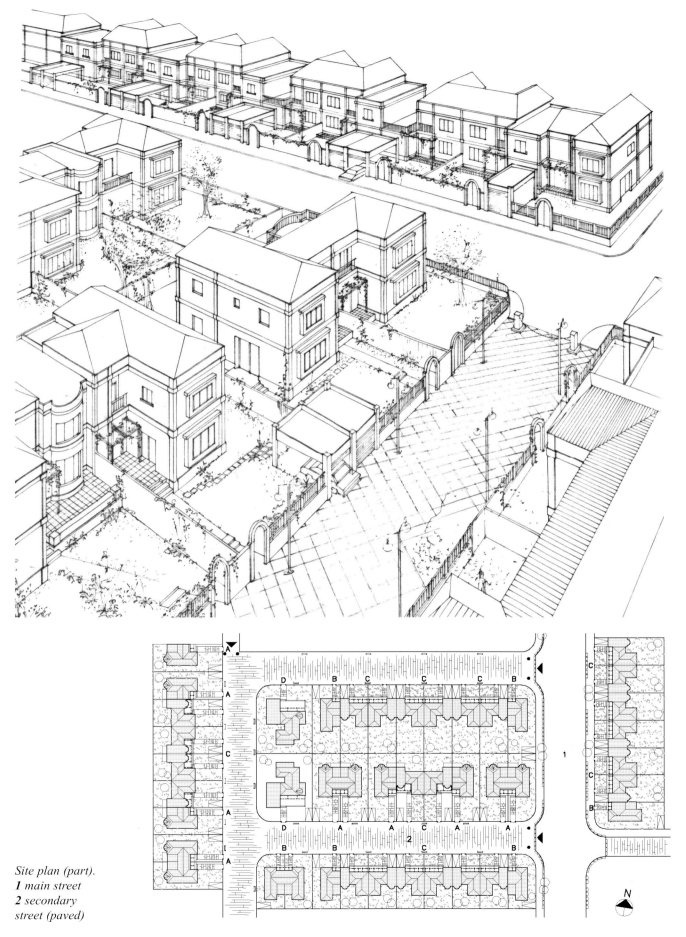

*Site plan (part).*
*1 main street*
*2 secondary*
*street (paved)*

149

Type A. When
the entrance to
the lot was from
the south or the
east, the garden
was located at the
front and type A
was developed
accordingly, so
that both the
house and the
garden will be
exposed to the
sun.

Ground-floor
plan (left) and
first-floor plan
(right).

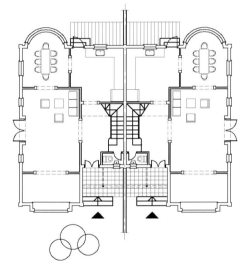
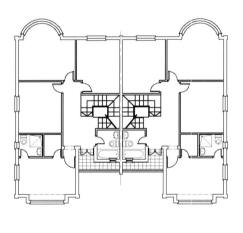

Type C – row
houses.

Ground-floor
plan (left) and
first-floor plan
(right).

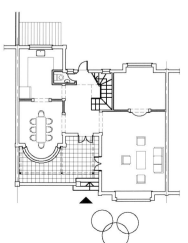
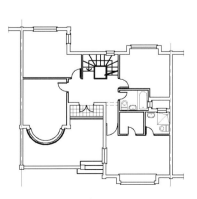

150

*Type B. When the entrance to the lot was from the north, the garden was located at the back and type B developed accordingly, so that both the house and the garden were exposed to the sun.*

*Ground-floor plan (left) and first-floor plan (right).*

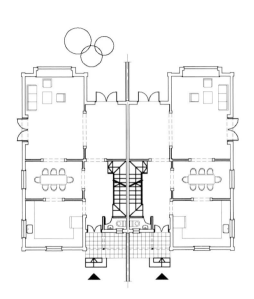

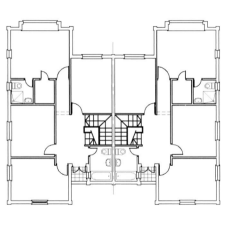

151

# Neighborhood center (shops, synagogue)

**Jerusalem, Israel**
**Completion date: shops 1987, synagogue 1995**

The neighborhood center includes shops, a synagogue and an open public square. Nestling in the heart of a residential area of white stone landscape, it is distinguished by its pink stone and red-tiled roofs.

The natural topographical lines of the sloped site determined the entrance level to the shops and to the synagogue as well as the landscaping levels.

The direction of the paths and the exact location of the shops and the synagogue on the site stemmed from a design process that took place on the site itself, while taking a slow walk from the upper level of the site to the lower one. This process led to locating the public square at the lower level and marking the paths according to the sequence of landmarks overlooking the outstanding scenery. The main path leads to the synagogue, and then splits into two routes. One route leads directly to the square, and the other turns into an arcade, which leads to the shops at the different levels of the site. The various paths intersect on different levels, allowing movement throughout the center.

*Marking the direction of the path and the borderlines of the building on the site was dictated by the scenery at the distance.*

152

Overall view of
the center.

Site plan.
**1** main gate to
the center from
upper level
**2** synagogue
**3** gates to syna-
gogue's court-
yard
**4** shops
**5** open square at
lower level
**6** arcade

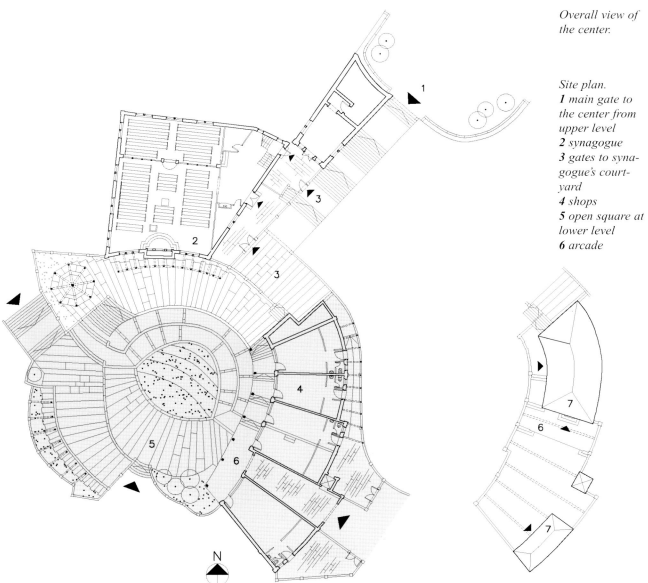

N

The difference in height between the synagogue's entrance terrace and the open square at the bottom of the site created a natural open amphitheater, where stone seats were planned.

An external stairway leads to the roof of the shops, where a café terrace offers a magnificent view of Jerusalem.

The buildings are of the traditional "Jerusalem stone", the inherent properties of which actually dictated the nature of the construction details which created the common language of the neighborhood center.

*View of the back façade (right). An arched gateway leads to the public square.*

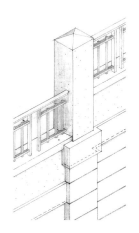

*Construction detail. The structural elements of the building, such as the periphery beam and column, are clearly distinguished.*

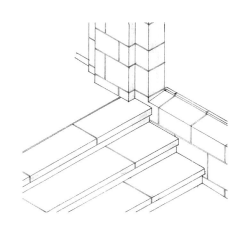

*Construction detail. The meeting point between the stone stairs, the windowsill and the column of the shopping arcade.*

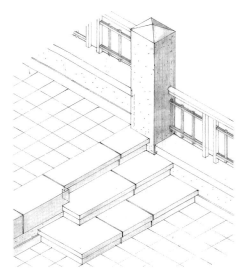

*Construction detail. The place where the stone stairs meet the railing wall at the roof terrace.*

154

The café opens to a roof terrace, facing the magnificent view of Jerusalem.

A traditional pattern of an entrance gate to second floor in Safad (right).

Stairs leading from synagogue's entrance terrace to roof terrace café (left).

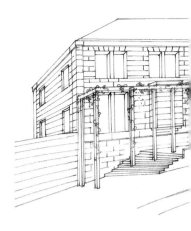

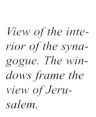

The interior design of the synagogue was based on traditional patterns. Being an Ashkenazic synagogue, the worshippers' seats were placed parallel to and opposite the Holy Ark, a pattern influenced by the seating arrangement in churches, with which Jews in their countries of origin were familiar. The wall of the Holy Ark is positioned in the direction of the Western Wall in the old city of Jerusalem. The highly impressive space includes the main prayer hall and the women's wing at the upper gallery. The worshippers can enjoy the beautiful scenery framed by the tall windows.

*The synagogue with the Holly Ark alcove facing Jerusalem.*

*View of the interior of the synagogue. The windows frame the view of Jerusalem.*

*Elevation drawing of the synagogue.*

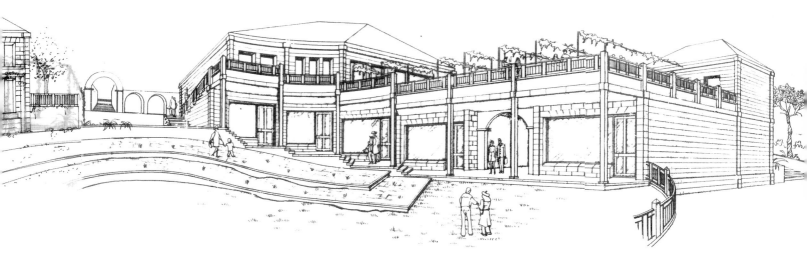

*Perspective drawing of the center.*

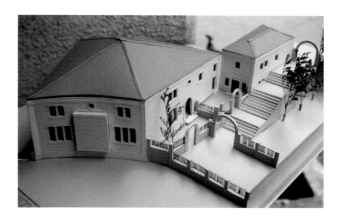

*Model of the synagogue.*

*View of the synagogue and the public square from the roof terrace.*

# Mobile markets

**Ramat Gan, Israel**
**Completion date: 1992**

**Maalot Tarshicha, Israel**
**Completion date: 1993**

**Eilat**
**Design phase: 1998**

A market is often associated with disorder and grime. My idea was to create a market which will not only offer a location for commercial activity, but will also become a venue for other types of entertainment and events in the urban landscape. Although the market had to be mobile and the stalls had to be provisional, it was important to convey a feeling of permanence, so as to radiate a strong sense of *a place* when the market was on site.

An open-arched gate marked the entrance to the market site. This important element generated the feeling of entering *the marketplace*.

The site plan located the stalls along "streets" and "squares". This repetitive pattern took a different form in accordance with the site conditions in each location.

The stalls themselves featured different shapes and sizes, and were made of modular steel elements that could be dismantled within minutes. This structural system enabled much flexibility and gave the dealers a wide variety of stalls of different sizes and types to choose from.

The stall's "roof" was made of folded parasols in different distinct colors, giving the stall the appearance of a "house".

This range of different elements, which repeated itself in various combinations, formed the architectural language of the market. The rainbow of colors, in combination with the exciting variety of goods, generated that special character and atmosphere of this unique type of a market.

*The gate is the element that generates the feeling of entering the market.*

*Different forms of stools, generating one architectural language, produce the feeling of the market.*

158

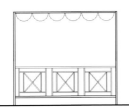

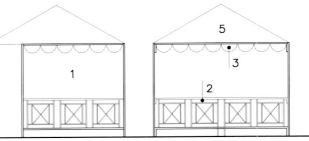

1  *Side element of individual stool*

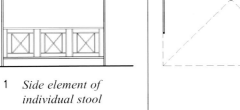

2  *Back bottom linkage between side elements*

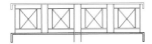

3  *Upper linkage between side elements*

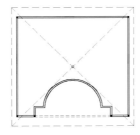

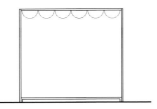

4  *Open side element creating a continuity between the stools*

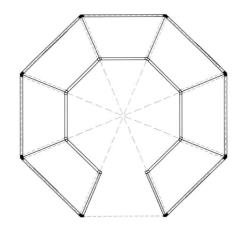
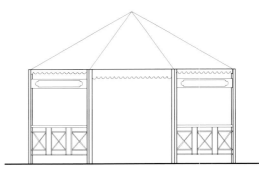

5  *Folding roofings in different colors*

*Type A. Open
stool with red
or green roof.*

*Type B. Table
stool with yel-
low roof.*

*Type C. Kiosk
with red roof.*

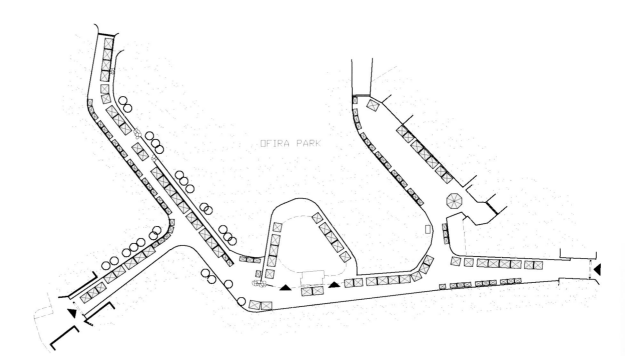

*Site plan of Ofira Park. Stools located along the park's paths.*

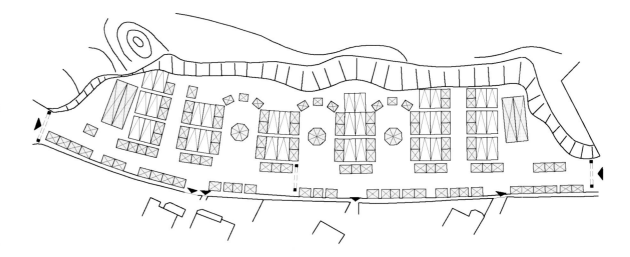

*Site plan of Maalot-Tarshicha. The plan is composed of small squares, each designed for a different kind of merchandise (fruit, vegetables, cloths), open to the main "street".*

*Overall view
of Ramat Gan
Market.*

*The market
as an entertain-
ment event.*

*Master plans*

# West Yefet Hatsorfim development
## Rebirth of old Jaffa

**Old Jaffa, Israel**
**Design phase: 1991–2004**

Jaffa, one of the most ancient cities in the world, whose remains can be traced back to the second century BC, has been destroyed and rebuilt many times. The hill of ancient Jaffa at the center of the city is surrounded by the remains of its ancient wall destroyed by Napoleon, and the natural port that used to be the gate to the Land of Israel. Jaffa was known for its oranges which earned international reputation.

The development compound is located along the ditch at the seam between the old and new city. The construction outside the old city walls began in the middle of the 19th century, under the Ottoman rule, when in a surge of urban development markets, administrative buildings, monasteries and transportation routes were constructed.

The objective of the new development plan was to revitalize the compound, which was in a rundown state, while realizing to the maximum the potential inherent in these beautiful buildings of such historic value.

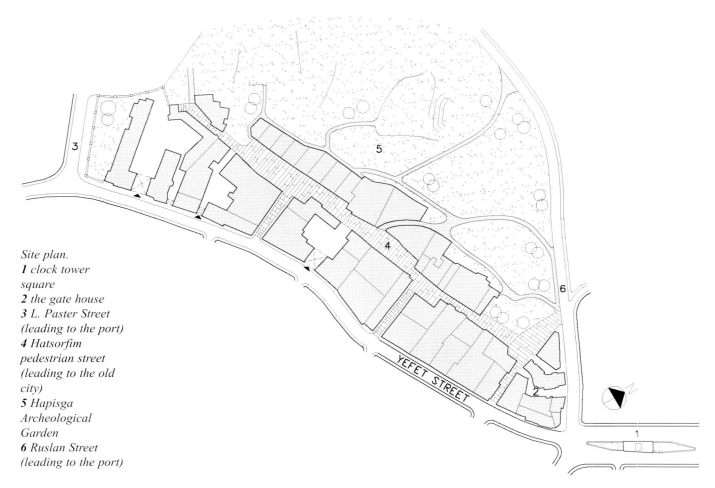

*Site plan.*
*1 clock tower square*
*2 the gate house*
*3 L. Paster Street (leading to the port)*
*4 Hatsorfim pedestrian street (leading to the old city)*
*5 Hapisga Archeological Garden*
*6 Ruslan Street (leading to the port)*

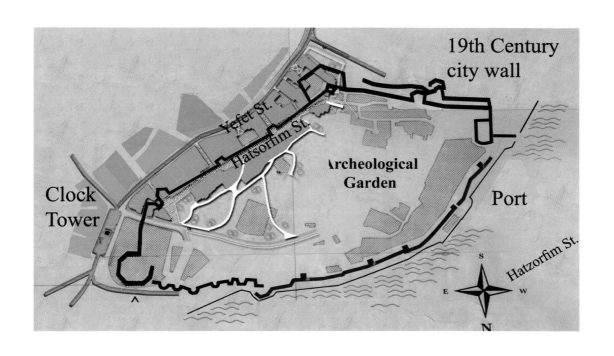

19th Century
city wall

Yefet St.

Hatsorfim St.

Archeological
Garden

Clock
Tower

Port

Hatzorfim St.

S

E        W

N

At the western boundary of the compound is the Hapisga Archeological Garden, the center of gravity of the old city of Jaffa. Here the remains of the Ra'amses Gate that dates back to the second century BC were found.

At the eastern boundary of the compound runs Yefet Street, which gives the impression of a *wadi*, a pattern that repeats itself in other ancient cities in the Mediterranean region, such as Siena or Venice, an impression I wanted to preserve and enhance in the new development plan.

The buildings that run along Yefet Street are the most magnificent ones left from the mid-19th century. Their walls are of regionally quarried sandstone, sometimes coated with colored plaster. Their ceilings are high and ornamental, the windows are arched, and the roofs are made of red clay tiles.

In contrast to the common conception, according to which the building's old façade is kept frozen and is totally disconnected from the new content behind it, thus turning it into a mere theatrical setting, here life was to be generated by creating a functional link between the building's new interior and its existing exterior.

*Yefet Street in its present state. We can preserve the historic environment if we create the conditions to assure its continuous life.*

*Yefet Street after renewal: perspective drawings and watercolor. A true dialogue between the historic fabric and the new construction.*

*Hapisga
Archeological
Garden (2nd
century BC).*

*View of the en-
trance to Yefet
Street from the
clock tower
square.*

 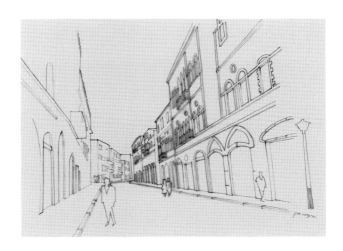

169

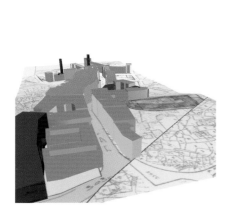
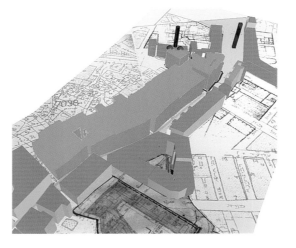
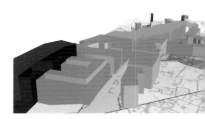

*Simulations
of the site after
development.*

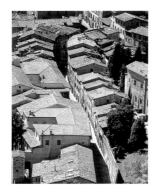

*Yefet Street feels
like a "wadi" –
a pattern I want-
ed to preserve
and enhance.*

*Traditional
pattern of
a "wadi" street.
Siena.*

*Gateway leading
from Yefet Street
through a court-
yard to Hatsor-
fim Street (19th
century).*

*Realizing to the
maximum the
potential inher-
ent in these 19th-
century monu-
mental buildings.*

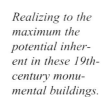

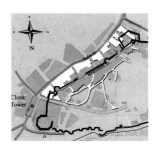

*The main entrance to Hatsorfim Street (right).*

*Hatsorfim Street in its present state characterized as a "casba" fabric.*

*New construction preserving the spirit of Hatsorfim Street.*

At the northern part of the compound, next to the clock square, we find the "Gate House" complex, with the ruins of the guard tower at the top. That house constitutes the main entrance to the old city of Jaffa. The "Gate House" complex, like the houses on Hatsorfim Street, is characterized by a "casba" fabric, having buildings with vaulted ceilings.

As opposed to other places, where ancient cities have been converted into static museums or sterile pilgrimage sites for tourists only, here an attempt was made to generate activity throughout the day by allowing residential, commercial and cultural uses. The idea was to create a dynamic urban area, where the

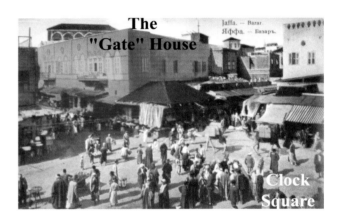

existing historic fabric is respected and preserved while newly built parts are added, with a balanced spread of the new construction.

*The Gate House street-level plan.*
■ *commercial*
■ *residential lobby*
□ *open courtyard and pathway*

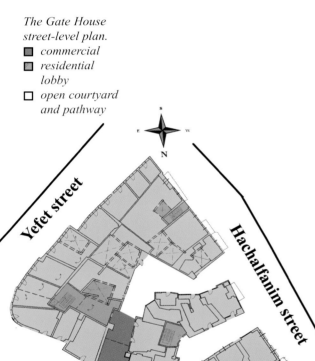

**The Old Gate Area**

**Yefet street**

**Hachalfanim street**

**Ruslan street**

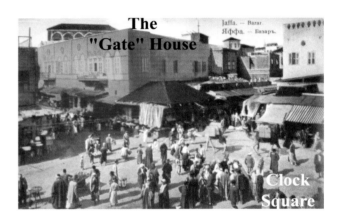

*Photograph (dated 1880) showing The Gate House (demolished), taken from the old market place at the entrance to Yefet Street, that later became the clock square.*

*View from the courtyard to the old gate.*

*Ruslan Street in its present state (right).*

172

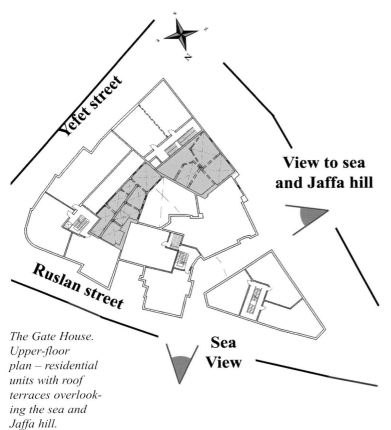

**View to sea and Jaffa hill**

**Sea View**

*The Gate House. Upper-floor plan – residential units with roof terraces overlooking the sea and Jaffa hill.*

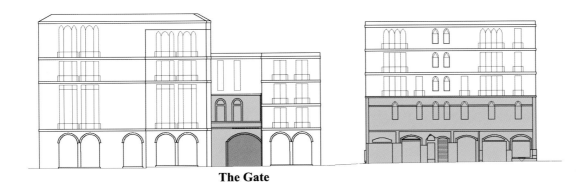

**The Gate**

*New elevation to Ruslan Street.*
■ *existing sand-stone wall for preservation*

173

# High-density housing

**Givatayim, Israel**
**Design phase: 1991; 2003**

A high-density large-scale residential neighborhood of 200 apartment units can seem threatening to the environment. That is why I sought a planning solution which would give the construction mass a friendly and welcoming appearance that would appeal both to the residents and the passersby.

The proposed solution was to divide the mass into two rows of apartment blocks with a park in-between. Instead of the common site plans, where buildings are laid out as autonomous fragments surrounded by useless green strips, here the outdoor areas were partly combined to form a semi-public park, and partly attached to the ground floor apartments as private gardens.

The front row of apartments faces both the street and the park, and the back row faces the park. In any event, all the apartments have access and view of the green public area. This layout is distinguished from most apartment buildings, where part of the apartments face the street and others face "nowhere".

As the façades of the buildings form the boundary that determines the character of the public area, maximum attention was given to the very small details that eventually constituted their whole. The façade was not perceived as a two dimensional, monolithic and alien entity, but rather as a complex combination of friendly construction details and materials, an approach normally taken only in small-scale houses.

The project consists of a variety of apartments, with only two apartment units sharing a lobby on each floor. The ground-floor apartments have private entrances from private gardens attached to them. The upper-floors have apartments of different sizes. The top floor apartments are designed as penthouses with roof terraces overlooking the city and the sea at the far distance.

*Site plan.*
*1 entrance to the apartment buildings*
*2 private entrance to ground-floor apartments*
*3 entrance to the back row of buildings and park*
*4 semi-public park*
*5 entrance to parking*
*6 shops*

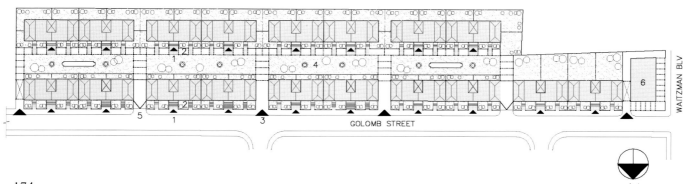

# Master plan for a residential neighborhood

**Mevaseret, Jerusalem, Israel**
**Design phase: 1986**

The site designated for this residential neighborhood was spread over the terraces on the hill facing the entrance road to Jerusalem. The project included some 60 plots on which one-family units or duplex houses were to be built at different times, by individual buyers.

My task was to prepare a set of building codes that would establish the layout of the streets, the size and boundaries of the plots, the location of the built areas on each plot, the size and height of the houses, and the types of building materials.

In most "Build Your own House" type of neighborhoods, building development is dictated by a rigid master plan that must be followed. Here an attempt was made to propose a dynamic planning process that would establish abstract common *planning rules* (instead of a fixed plan) relating to the structure of the neighborhood as a whole, the structure of each plot and the house itself, so that like in traditional villages, although the houses might look different, and so will the neighborhood as a whole, they will "speak" the same language. These rules were to define and ensure the desirable qualitative relationships among the various components of the neighborhood. Each stage of construction, whether a street or a house, was to be guided by the common rules, interacting with the physical reality that would develop on the site itself at *that time*.

Thus the initial stage of planning was in fact a model of a process to be followed by subsequent stages in the future.

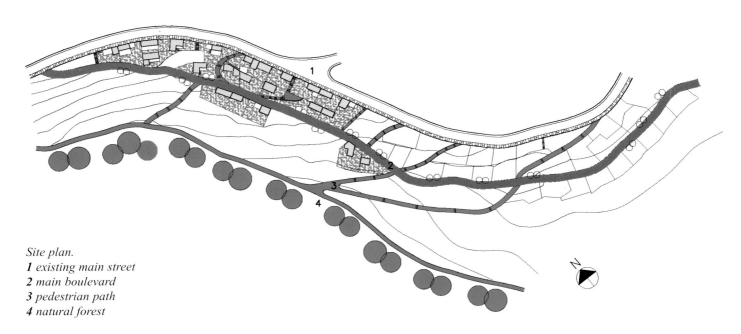

*Site plan.*
*1 existing main street*
*2 main boulevard*
*3 pedestrian path*
*4 natural forest*

*Overall view of the site facing the entrance road to Jerusalem. The boulevards and the paths follow those trodden by the villagers prior to my arrival.*

*The route of the path, determined on the site itself.*

177

The abstract patterns established on different sites, with varied environmental conditions, ultimately produced the variety of forms and houses and the non-uniformity of the different parts of the neighborhood.

Along the topographic lines, a main boulevard was drawn which bisected the neighborhood. Intersecting with it were the secondary roads that led the pedestrians from inside the neighborhood to the forest along its boundaries. The route of the boulevard and the smaller paths were established while walking through the area, attempting to follow the paths that had been trodden by the villagers prior to our arrival.

Unlike the common planning process, by which the boundaries of plots are set arbitrarily and mechanically, without any attention to the natural conditions and qualities of the site, and the houses are located accordingly, here the boundaries of each plot stemmed from the layout of the building and were drawn accordingly. The exact location of the built area on the plot and the location of the outdoor spaces were determined on the basis of very definite criteria: allowing the southern sun to penetrate the house through the garden, leaving open spaces exposed to the scenery and allocating the part of the site where the incline was relatively moderate for the gardens.

This kind of a planning process produced a non-standard and organic shape of plots, in harmony with the natural terrain.

*The position of the path in-between existing trees.*

The relative size of the built space and open garden area on each plot, as well as their interrelation with the street, changed from one plot to another, according to the character we wished to attribute to any specific street or lane. On the main boulevard, which was to have a more "urban" character, the boundary with the street was designed as a "wall", bringing the house line to the street, with the garden partially exposed. On the secondary roads, which were to have a more "rural" character, the boundary with the street was marked by a low railing that almost totally exposed the garden.

On the whole the intention was to echo in the design of the new neighbourhood the spirit of the beautiful villages built through the ages at the outskirts of Jerusalem, close to this neighborhood.

*The boundaries of each plot stemmed organically from the predetermined position of the built and outdoor areas.*

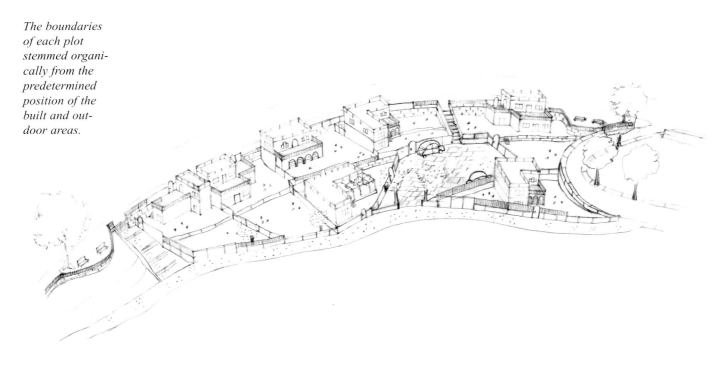

*Perspective view of the main boulevard. The boundaries with the street were designed as a "wall".*

*Perspective view of the path facing the forest. The boundaries with the forest were designed as a bench.*

*Perspective view of the secondary road. The boundaries with the street allow the exposure of the private gardens.*

179

# Ramat Amidar renewal project

**Ramat Gan, Israel**
**Design phase: 1982**

The secret of success of any physical plan of a neighborhood lies in its perception as part of a wider system, that embodies its physical, social and economic structure, a comprehensive plan that enables to realize to the maximum the potential inherent in the neighborhood. The aim of the project was to create in the Ramat Amidar neighborhood a system that will enable its community to build and revitalize its communal life as well as the private life of its inhabitants.

The plan was based on a model that was initially developed by the "Center for Environmental Structure", Berkeley, for North Omaha, USA (1981).

Although such a plan is physical in essence, dealing with roads, houses and public buildings, I was aware of the fact that the role of any renewal program is first and foremost to bring life to the neighborhood. In order to do so it is necessary to initiate an ongoing process of social awareness and alertness to the problems created in the neighborhood, that will motivate people to fortify their environment. However, social awareness is not enough. Motivation and aspiration to a better life are subject to the economic strengthening of the neighborhood, so that more people will work and reinvest their earned money in the neighborhood and thus contribute to its physical renewal.

Unlike existing planning processes by which renewal of a neighborhood is carried out according to a static master plan that tries to foresee a future reality and thus makes decisions that will probably be irrelevant when implemented, here an attempt was made to create a dynamic planning process which the community will adopt and use in order to determine its physical future along time, in an ever-changing reality. To this end the following method was introduced: A set of codes was formulated in cooperation with the inhabitants of the neighborhood, specifying the

*Perspective view of the neighborhood as a whole after renewal.*

principles that will govern the development of the neighborhood and ensure its quality in years to come. The planning rules as well as the structure of the neighborhood were conceived as a hierarchical system with the rules relating to each of the four structural levels of the neighborhood:

a. the neighborhood as a whole;

b. the sub-neighborhood (together the sub-neighborhoods create the neighborhood);

c. a group of buildings (together the groups create the sub-neighborhood).

180

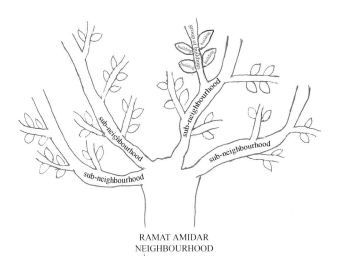

The neighbor-
hood is con-
ceived as a hier-
archical system.

group of buildings

building building

building building

sub-neighbourhood

sub-neighbourhood

sub-neighbourhood

sub-neighbourhood

RAMAT AMIDAR
NEIGHBOURHOOD

Overall view
of the neighbor-
hood before re-
newal.

181

The rules for the level of the *neighborhood as a whole* specified the principles for defining and reinforcing its borders, promoting its commercial and cultural centers and improving the internal roads connecting these activity centers.

The rules for the *sub-neighborhood* level specified the principles for promoting its activity centers, defining its identity and borders and addressing issues like pedestrian alleys.

*The street before renewal.*

*Perspective view of the street (sub-neighborhood level) after renewal. Defined boundaries between the private and public domains.*

*The commercial street before renewal.*

182

*Neighborhood plan.*

**1–14**  sub-neighbour-
hoods

boundaries of
subneighbour-
hoods

public building

main streets
connecting
public nodes

pedestrian lane

12

11

13

9

10

8

14

6

2

7

5

4

1

3

N

BAR-ILAN
UNIVERSITY

*Perspective view
of the commer-
cial node. The
renewed façade
creates a lively
dialogue be-
tween the build-
ing and the
street.*

The rules for the *group of buildings* level specified the principles for establishing land ownership, border lines between private and public open spaces and addressed issues such as the façade of buildings and the creation of transition areas from the street to the entrance to the buildings.

*Group of buildings before renewal.*

*Perspective view of a group of buildings after renewal.*

*Defining the boundaries of land ownership establishes healthy relations between the building and its outdoor space.*

The rules for the *individual building* specified the position of the new building additions in relation to the allocation of areas for private gardens, keeping the outdoor spaces open to the sun. The rules also addressed issues such as uniform building materials.

In any renewal process an organic order can emerge only if the process is gradual and the development and rehabilitation grows out of the daily reality in the neighborhood. For that purpose any planning decision must be taken on the basis of a diagnostic map drawn currently by the community and the planner of each part of the neighborhood.

Representatives of the inhabitants will be responsible for determining the extent to which those established rules have been followed, and where improvement is called for, always keeping in mind both the specific level of the neighborhood they represent and the larger level of the neighborhood it contributes to as a whole.

For example, if a suggestion is made at the *neighborhood level* to build a senior-citizens center, the diagnostic map of the neighborhood as a whole will enable to determine the best place for its location, that "weak" place that will most benefit from the new project, thus strengthening it and the neighborhood as a whole.

The budgeting principle will also ensure a balanced distribution of resources. Each level of scale in the renewal project will be allocated a fixed relative sum, and although the overall development budget may change, the relative part of the budget for each level will stay constant, preserving the balance.

This organic approach, by which the organizational structure of the neighborhood, the planning rules and the budget allocation are regarded as a system in which the interrelations between the parts on every level of scale are mutually contributive, will ensure a healthy and wholesome renewal.

*Perspective view after renewal. Establishing the interrelation between the building and its outdoors.*

*The individual building before renewal. The outdoor areas are no man's land, with no feeling of passing from the public to the private domain.*

*Perspective view. Newly created transition area that both connects and separates the building and the street.*

*Private houses*

# Shutz residence
## The House Around the Lemon Tree

**Jerusalem, Israel**
**Completion date: 1978**

The home of the writer David Shutz was built in a typical Jerusalem neighborhood, where beautiful stone buildings were constructed in the early 20th century. This was my first commission as an architect, starting my own office.

I was asked to plan a new addition to the old small building and the courtyard adjacent to it. Neighboring buildings surrounded the courtyard, between which was the entrance gate from the main street. At the center of the courtyard there stood a lemon tree that played a significant role in the planning process.

The planning and creation of the outdoor space on the plot was conducted simultaneously with the planning of the new addition. The objective was to ensure that the lemon tree, which inspired the building's atmosphere, would have the living space it needs to continue to flourish. To establish that, I walked back and forth in the courtyard together with the owner, until we felt we had found *precisely* the right size for the patio. Such a planning process enables to discern that even a diversion of 10 cm could significantly change the feeling of this patio. I marked the boundaries of the courtyard with red chalk, and those became the boundaries of the new building addition.

Two beautiful old rooms, with vaulted ceiling and thick stonewalls facing the courtyard, were converted into a living room and kitchen. Alcoves that had been walled in over the years were reopened. The stone, which framed the inside doors and the alcoves and had been plastered over the years, was exposed. The new entrance hall was the space which both connected and separated the new and the old, functioning as a transition area between the courtyard and the house. The master bedroom and study were located at the new wing, facing the view of the courtyard.

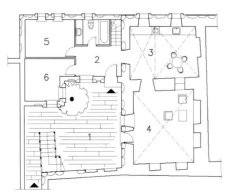

*Ground-floor plan.*
*1 entrance courtyard*
*2 entrance hall*
*3 kitchen and dining room*
*4 living room (old building)*
*5 bedroom*
*6 bedroom*

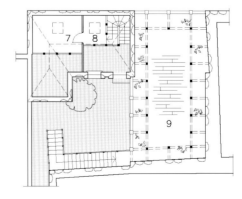

*First-floor plan.*
*7 master bedroom*
*8 study room*
*9 roof terrace (access from the courtyard)*

*View of the new building addition with the main-entrance door.*

*The building lines of the house (in relation to the lemon tree) were constructed on the chalk marks (planning decision) previously made on the site itself.*

*The living room with its vaulted ceiling and thick stonewall is located in the old building, facing the court-yard.*

An open stairway led from the courtyard to the building's roof, a pattern that was widespread in Mediterranean building tradition. The roof, that traditionally served as sleeping quarters on hot summer nights and for the drying of spices, was converted into a roof terrace with a view of the courtyard and vine trellis on the sides. The architectural language I used for the new addition was an echo of the traditional language of stone houses built in Jerusalem, derived from the type and nature of the stone itself.

*The stones which had originally framed the alcove in the kitchen-dining area and then covered with plaster, were now exposed.*

*Open stairway
leading from the
courtyard to the
roof terrace.*

# Three houses

**Zichron Ya'akov, Israel**

**Ben Abraham residence**
Completion date: 1990

**Portugali residence**
Completion date: 1991

**David residence**
Completion date: 1999

The approach underlying my design of three houses on the rocky hills of Zichron Ya'akov was that a building must grow naturally from the site on which it is built, and not force itself upon it.

The process by which the planning decisions were taken on the site was preceded by a study of both the quantitative and qualitative needs specified by the families for whom the three houses were designed. These needs were translated into a list of "patterns", which abstractly but specifically defined the spatial order of the houses.

The three houses, built on the basis of *similar patterns,* came out *different in form*. The plans of the buildings developed gradually from the deep interaction between those similar patterns and the living reality of the actual site, a reality that *differed* from site to site.

The three different houses will be presented by way of an analysis of that list of similar patterns that were applied to all, illustrating the above-mentioned approach. The names of the patterns and the quotations are taken from the book *A Pattern Language.*

*Ben Abraham residence.*
*Portugali residence.*
*David residence.*

194

*Ben Abraham residence.*

## Entrance gate

One of the first decisions concerning the house involves the location of the entrance gate to the site. This location determines the relationship between the house and the street. While walking up and down the street, I searched intuitively for the most natural place to enter the site.

*Ben Abraham
residence.*

# Site repair

"Consider the site and its building as a single living ecosystem. Leave those areas that are the most precious, beautiful, comfortable, and healthy as they are; and build new structures in those parts of the site, which are least pleasant now." I stayed at the site for hours, trying to feel its various areas. The spot where I wanted to sit a long while was left as an open space for the veranda.

*David residence.*

*Ben Abraham residence.*

## South-facing outdoors

"Place the building to the north of the outdoor spaces that go with them. And keep the outdoor spaces to the south (sun). Never leave a deep band of shade between the building and the sunny part of the outdoors." Here there was a conflict between the preferable direction of the view and the direction of the sun, the priorities were weighed on a case-by-case basis.

*Portugali resi-
dence.*

## Main-entrance door

Once the location of the entrance gate and the built-up
areas on the site were marked on the ground, the next
search, perhaps the most important one in the evolution
of the plan, was for the proper location of the entrance
door. "Place the main entrance of the building at a
point where it can be seen immediately from the main
avenues of approach and give it a bold, visible shape
which stands out in front of the building."

*Ben Abraham
residence.*

*David residence
(left).*

## The location of the different activities within the built-up area

Once the rough boundaries of the built-up areas were marked and the position of the main-entrance door was "located", the location of each space within those boundaries was determined by the qualities intended for that space. For example, the living room, the life core of the house, where the family spends relatively more time, was located in direct relation to the garden and the more serene view. The dining room, the entrance hall and interior passages, where one would spend relatively less time, were placed in relation to the more dramatic views seen from the site.

*Ben Abraham residence. The position of the dining-room window was determined on the site, to frame the view of the Atlit fortress at the far distance.*

# Wings of light

"Arrange the building so it breaks down into wings that correspond to the natural social groups (activity) within the building. Make each wing no more than 8 meters wide. So that natural day light will cover all areas of the house."

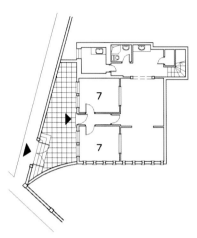
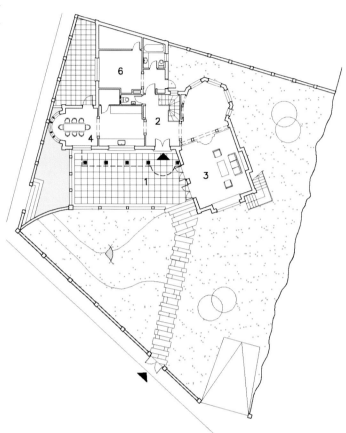

*Ben Abraham residence. Ground-floor plan (right). Lower ground-floor plan (left.)*

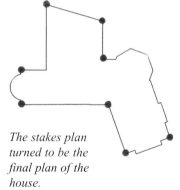

*The stakes plan turned to be the final plan of the house.*

*Each planning decision taken on the site stemmed from the whole created by previous ones.*

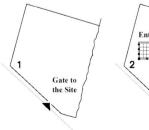
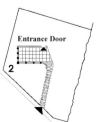
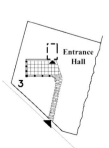

*David residence.
Ground-floor plan
(left) and first-
floor plan (right).*
*1 entrance gate*
*2 entrance hall*
*3 living room*
*4 dining room*
*5 guest room*
*6 master bedroom*
*7 children's rooms*
*8 balcony*

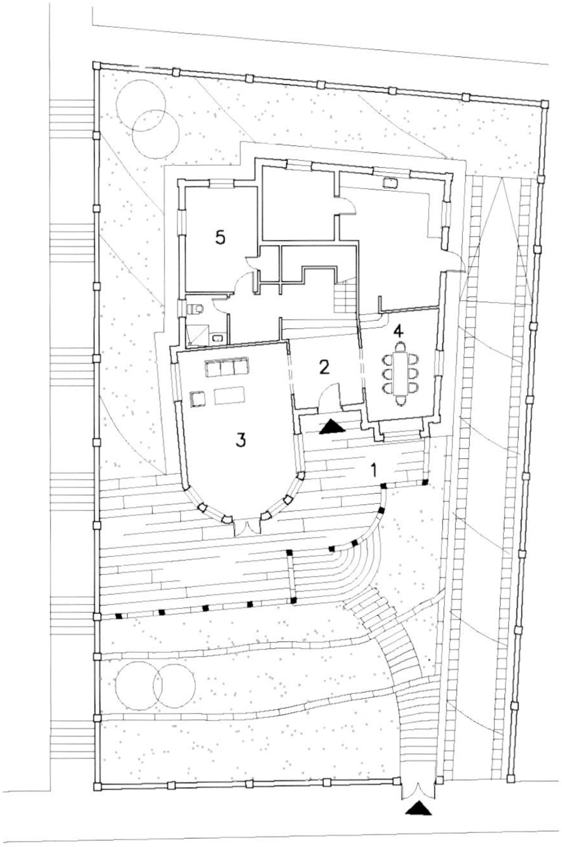

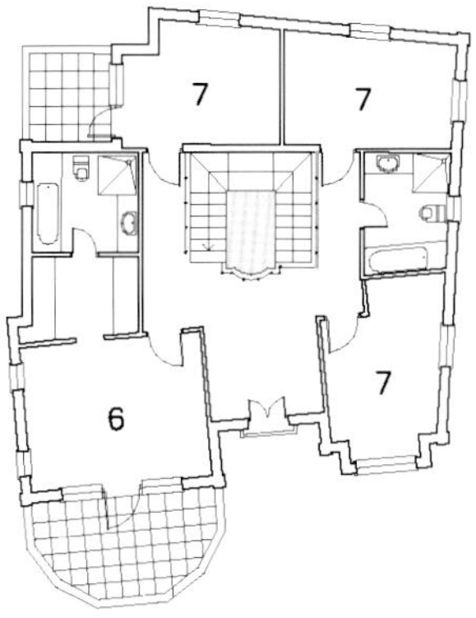

*Portugali resi-
dence. Ground-
floor plan.*

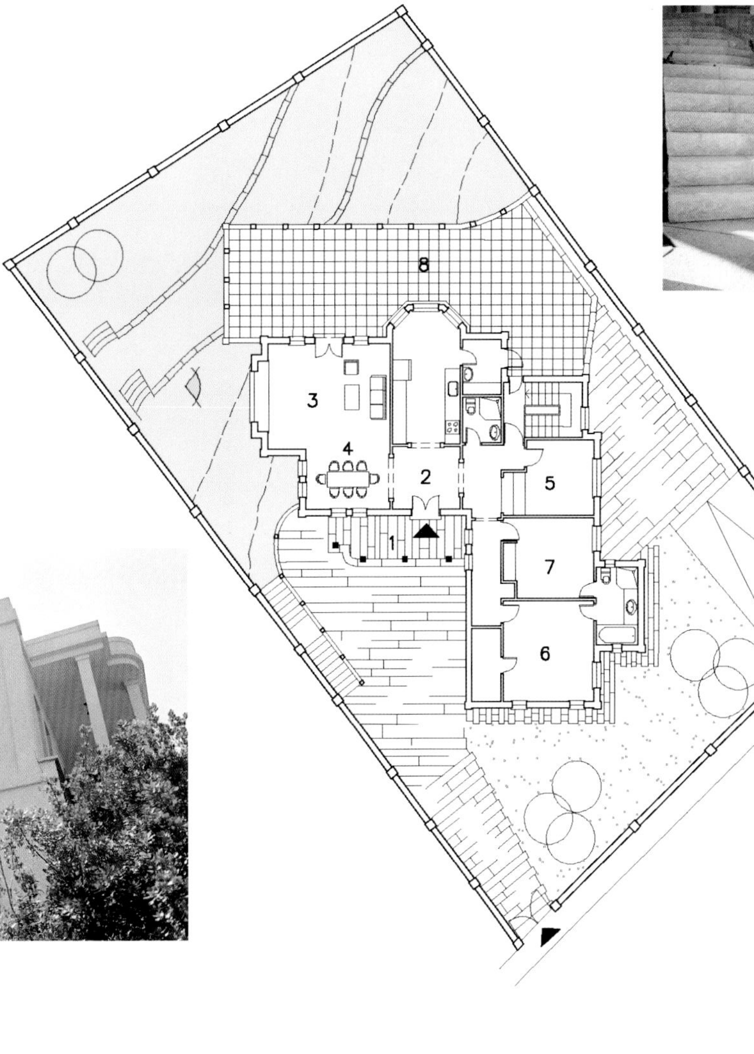

*Living and din-
ing areas facing
the sea view.*

203

# Entrance transition

"Make a transition space between the street and the front door. Mark it with a change of direction, a change of surface ... and above all a change of view."

*Portugali residence.*

*David residence.*

*Ben Abraham residence.*

# The flow through rooms

"The movement between the rooms is as important as the rooms themselves ... Avoid the use of corridors ... use public rooms and common rooms as rooms for movement ... give this indoor circulation from room to room a feeling of great generosity."

*David residence. The entrance hall is the space which both connects and separates the different activity rooms within the house (right).*

*David residence. Entrance space leading to the different bedrooms at the upper floor.*

*Portugali residence. The entrance hall and the space leading to the bedrooms that open from it, both give a generous feeling.*

*David residence. View of the entrance hall through the arch of the dining area. The red terrazzo used for the floor frame, the stairs and the panels link the different areas.*

## Staircase as a stage

"A staircase is not just a way of getting from one floor to another ... Treat the whole staircase as a room, so people coming down (or up) become part of the action ..."

## Focused view

"Where there are particularly beautiful views, do not destroy them by building one large picture window that turns the view into nondescript wallpaper. Special views should be framed and thereby intensified."

As experience has shown me that placing the window in a deviation of even 10 cm can violate all it is meant to achieve, the precise location of the window can be ascertained only by being *on the site itself.*

*David residence. Framing the hill in front of the bedroom.*

*Ben Abraham residence. The cliff at the edge of the site was left untouched and was later framed by the window.*

# Toch residence 1

**Jerusalem, Israel**
**Completion date: 1979**

The planning decision at the end of which the two-rooms apartment turned into a three-rooms apartment was to excavate and lower the apartment's ground floor level and bring it to the level of the attached garden, which was one meter below it. This addition to the original unusual height of the house (typical to the old houses of Jerusalem) enabled the creation of an additional floor, thus significantly extending the apartment's area.

The front room facing the street, which served as the living room, remained unchanged and so were its tall windows and decorated floor tiles. Alongside this room we installed several stairs that led to the excavated level, where we placed the kitchen and dining room, enabling direct access from there to the garden. The children's bedroom was located at the back of this level.

A new stairway was constructed from the entrance hall to the newly created second floor. This floor was built as an open gallery overlooking the living room, serving as the master bedroom and study area. The high windows of the living room offer a view of the garden and enable the filtering of daylight to all parts of the house.

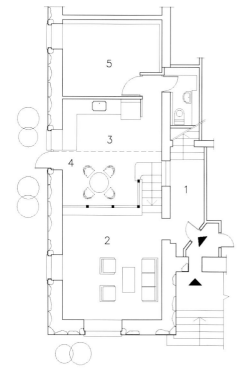

*Ground-floor plan.*
*1 entrance hall (existing floor level)*
*2 living room (existing floor level)*
*3 dining room – kitchen (excavated area)*
*4 new access to garden*
*5 bedroom (excavated area)*

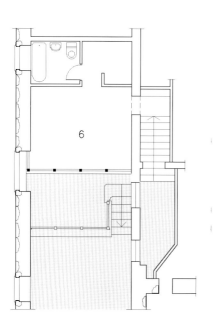

*Gallery-floor plan.*
*6 master bedroom and study area*

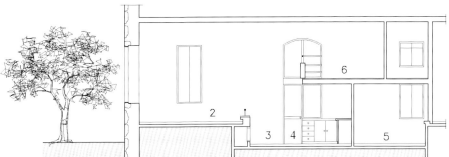

*Longitudinal
section.*

2     6     3   4     5

*View to entrance hall at existing floor level leading to excavated level.*

*A new door opened to the garden level after excavating indoors.*

*Old decorative tiles in the living room.*

# Toch residence 2

**Jerusalem, Israel**
**Completion date: 1995**

*A visual continuity between the entrance courtyard, the indoor spaces and the main garden at the back.*

The house we renovated was one of the most beautiful stone houses in a typical Jerusalem neighborhood.

In order to preserve an existing historical environment or a building, conditions must be created that will assure its continuous life. Thus, the key question in re-planning and restoring the house was, what design patterns will create a real dialogue between the spirit of the house, which I wanted to preserve, and the new and comfortable living conditions I wanted to provide.

The existing house was detached from the open areas adjacent to it. The windows were few and there was no access to the garden. The main entrance to the house was exposed to the street, having no protective entrance courtyard. The interior was divided by walls that blocked the inside spaces from the windows and the outside daylight.

The first step in the planning process was to apply those patterns that form the relationship between the house and the street. Then came the re-planning of the house itself, down to the very small construction details.

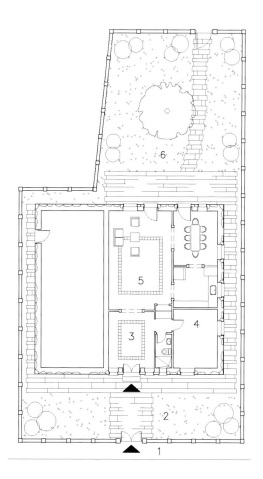

*Floor plan.*
*1 main street*
*2 entrance courtyard*
*3 entrance hall*
*4 bedroom*
*5 living room*
*6 garden*

214

In the "new" house, a wall was built at the front, creating an *entrance courtyard* which both separated the house from the street and connected it to it. It is a pattern that repeats itself in all traditional houses in Jerusalem.

Behind the entrance courtyard and clearly visible from the street, is the *main-entrance door*.

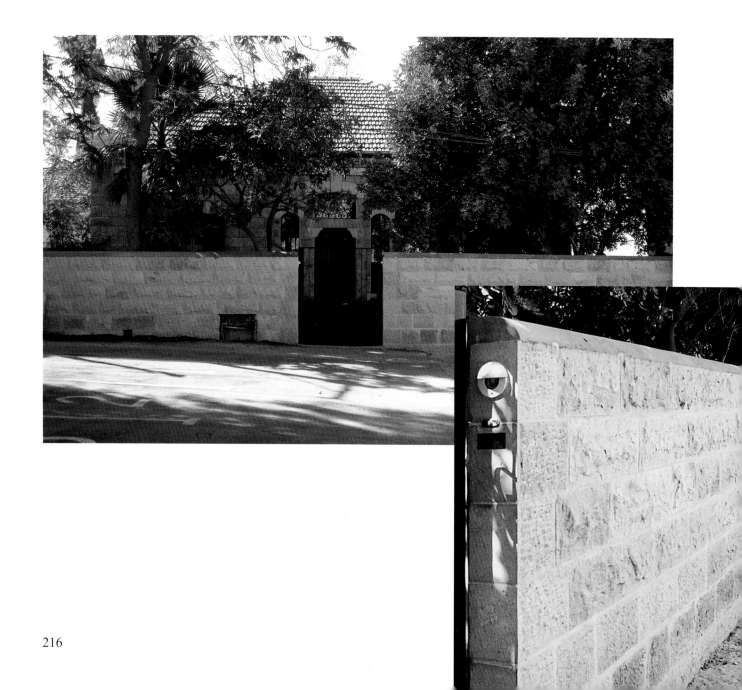

Behind the door there is an *entrance hall,* forming a transition area from the entrance courtyard to the interior of the house.

The plan of the house designated all the given area for the functional spaces without any use of corridors, thus creating a *sequence of spaces* that opened one onto the other, maintaining visual and movement continuity between the entrance courtyard, the entrance hall, the living room and the main garden at the back. Despite this feeling of continuity between the spaces, each space was clearly defined, having its own physical boundaries, with a distinct *entrance gate* that forms a threshold between one space and another.

*Entrance hall. The panel along the wall is an entity by itself both separating and connecting the wall and the floor.*

*The sunshine filtering into the house produces a golden light when it hits the yellow painted walls.*

*Sequence of spaces that open one onto the other.*

*The construction of the old ceiling was exposed and preserved.*

*Persian pattern printed on the ceramic tiles of the kitchen and bathroom.*

220

The kitchen and
dining room are
both connected
and separated
by a "gate".

The garden, which was concealed prior to the renovation, became an integral and vital part of the house, as new windows and doors were opened onto it. The new openings were made of steel, a material that matched the original old metal latticework in the house. The sunshine filtering into the house produced a golden light when it hit the yellow painted walls. Much of the renovation process focused on the details, both old ones that were exposed and preserved, or new ones, echoing the *spirit* of the preexisting architectural language of the neighborhood as a whole and the house in particular.

*The garden, which was concealed prior to the renovation, became an integral part of the house, as new windows and doors were opened onto it.*

*View to the new door and window opened from the dining room onto the garden.*

222

The old tiles in
the house were
reconstructed
and laid on the
new porch, form-
ing a transition
area between the
indoors and the
garden.

# Visual chronology of projects and buildings 1973–2005

**Shutz residence**
The House Around the Lemon Tree
Jerusalem, Israel
Completion date: 1978

**Toch residence 1**
Jerusalem, Israel
Completion date: 1979

**Memorial Site for the Fallen Intelligence Servicemen**
Glilot, Tel Aviv, Israel
Competition entry: 1982 – purchase prize

**Master plan for a neighorhood renewal**
Ramat Amidar, Ramat Gan, Israel
Design phase: 1982

**Steinbaum residence**
Jerusalem, Israel
Completion date: 1982

**Bar-restaurant**
Conversion of the old railway station
Jerusalem, Israel
Design phase: 1982

**Bar-restaurant**
Conversion of a 19th-century building
Jerusalem, Israel
Design phase: 1982

**Village centers renewal project**

Bnei Re'em, Israel
Design phase: 1983

Neve Mivtach, Israel
Design phase: 1983

**Idea model for community villages**
Competition entry: 1984 – purchase
prize

**Welfare central bureau**
Tel Aviv, Israel
Design phase: 1984

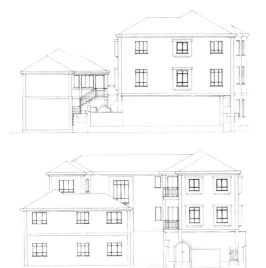

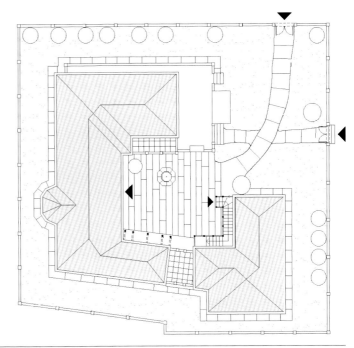

**Residential neighborhood**
Kibbutz Givat Haim Ichud, Israel
Design phase: 1985

**Master plan for a residential
neighborhood**
Mevaseret, Jerusalem, Israel
Design phase: 1986

**Apartment house**
Givatayim, Israel
Design phase: 1986

**Neighborhood center**
(shops, synagogue)
Jerusalem, Israel
Completion date: 1987 (shops),
1995 (synagogue)

**Residential cluster**
Jerusalem, Israel
Design phase: 1987

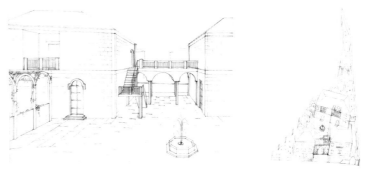

**Housing project**
Pisgat Zeev, Jerusalem, Israel
Design phase: 1987

226

**Children's day center**
Tel Aviv, Israel
Design phase: 1988

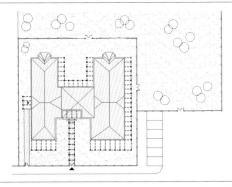

**Senior-citizens day center**
Tel Aviv, Israel
Completion date: 1988

**"Villas City" residential neighborhood**
Rishon Lezion, Israel
Competition entry: 1988 – first prize

**House for the elderly and commercial center**
Rishon Lezion, Israel
Competition entry: 1988

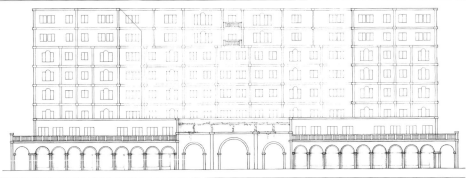

**Memorial site**
Eshtaol Forest, Judea Mountains, Israel
Design phase: 1988

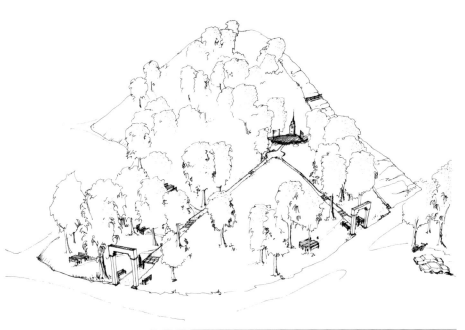

**The Maimonides Central Sephardic
Synagogue**
Hadera, Israel
Competition entry: 1988 – first prize
Design phase: 1988

**Housing project**
Tiberias, Israel
Design Phase: 1989

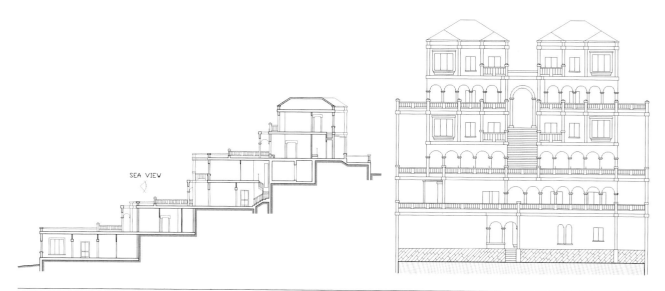

SEA VIEW

**Residential neighborhood**
Tiberias, Israel
Design phase: 1989

**Spiritual center**
(synagogue, yeshiva)
Kiryat Shmone, Israel
Design phase: 1989

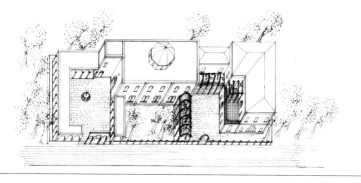

**Hochman residence**
Kiryat Ono, Israel
Completion date: 1990

**Jewish comprehensive school**
Charlottenburg, Berlin, Germany
Competition entry: 1990

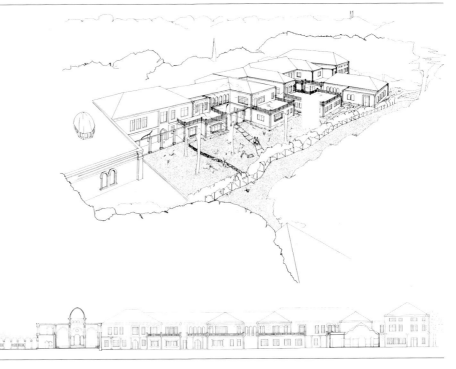

**City square**
Kiryat Shmone, Israel
Competition entry: 1990

**Ben Abraham residence**
Zichron Ya'akov, Israel
Completion date: 1990

**Shtemler residence**
Caesarea, Israel
Design phase: 1990

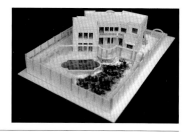

**Music library**
Beit Ariela central city library,
Tel Aviv, Israel
Completion date: 1991

**West Yefet Hatsorfim development**
Old Jaffa, Israel
Design phase: 1991–2004

**Post office – conversion**
Givatayim, Israel
Completion date: 1991

**Portugali residence**
Zichron Ya'akov, Israel
Completion date: 1991

**High-density housing**
Givatayim, Israel
Design phase: 1991; 2003

**Mobile markets**

Ramat Gan, Israel
Completion date: 1992

Maalot Tarshicha, Israel
Completion date: 1993

Eilat, Israel
Design phase: 1998

**Laor residence**
Kinneret, Israel
Design phase: 1992

**Town-hall extension**
Ramat Gan, Israel
Design phase: 1992

**Health clinic**
Givatayim, Israel
Design phase: 1993

**Housing renewal**
Beer Sheba, Israel
Design phase: 1993

**Senior-citizens day center**
Eilat, Israel
Competition entry: 1993

**Community center**
Or Akiva, Israel
Competition entry: 1994

**Senior-citizens day center**
Kfar Saba, Israel
Competition entry: 1994

**Toch residence 2**
Jerusalem, Israel
Completion date: 1995

**Community center for the arts**
Ashkelon, Israel
Design phase: 1995

**The Israel National War**
**Memorial Center**
Mount Eitan, Jerusalem, Israel
Competition entry: 1995

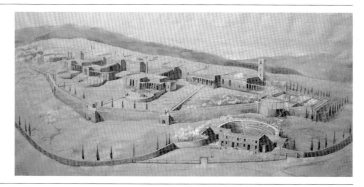

**Israel Defence Forces**
**Veterans Center**
Ramat-Gan, Israel
Competition entry: 1995, first price

**Residential neighborhood**
Kfar Yona, Israel
Competition entry: 1995

**Residential neighborhood**
Beit Dagan, Israel
Competition entry: 1996

**Lofts**
(apartments, shops)
Jaffa, Israel
Design phase: 1996

**Shopping mall**
Dimona, Israel
Competition entry: 1996

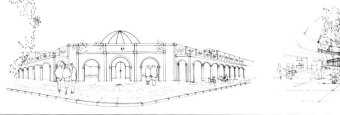

**Ohel Shem community and school library**
Ohel Shem High School, Ramat Gan, Israel
Completion date: 1996

**Music center and library**
Tel Aviv, Israel
Completion date: 1997

**International Center for the Study of Bird Migration and Field Study School**
Armored Corps Memorial Site, Latrun, Israel
Design phase: 1997

**Tselermayer residence**
Caesarea, Israel
Design phase: 1998

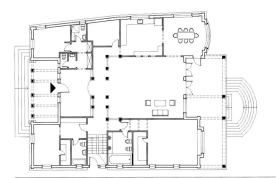

**Cafeteria pavilion**
Blich High School, Ramat Gan,
Israel
Design phase: 1998

**Grant residence**
Herzelia Pituach, Israel
Design phase: 1998

**Cultural center and library**
Kibbutz Mishmar Haemek, Israel
Design phase: 1999

**Commercial and leisure center**
Reem Junction, Israel
Design phase: 1999

**Central city library and resource center**
Haifa, Israel
Competition entry: 1999

**David residence**
Zichron Ya'akov, Israel
Completion date: 1999

**Glik apartment – conversion**
Tel Aviv, Israel
Completion date: 2000

**The Khan Heritage Center
and Center for the Arts**
Hadera, Israel
Design phase: 2000

**Residential neighborhood in a
kibbutz**
Kibbutz Maagan Michael, Israel
Completion date: stage 1 2001,
stage 2 2005

**Central city library**
Ramat Gan, Israel
Design phase: 2001

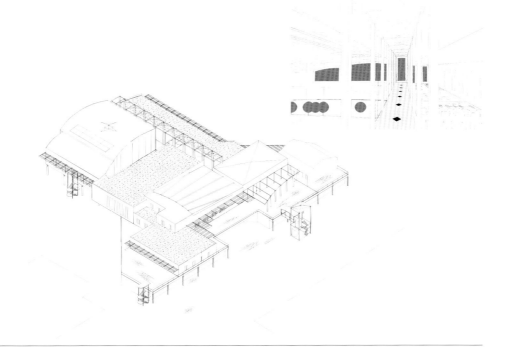

**Student dormitories**
Technion Institute of Technology,
Haifa, Israel
Competition entry: 2001

**Senior-citizens day center**
Hadera, Israel
Competition entry: 2002

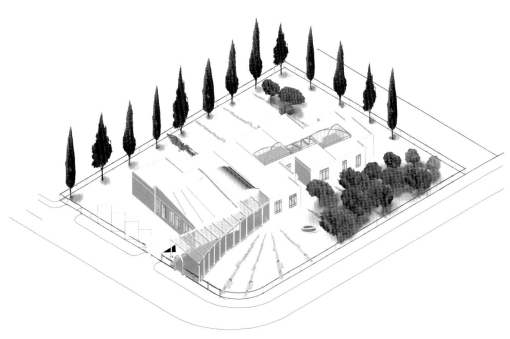

**Ir Yamim community center**
Natanya, Israel
Design phase: 2004

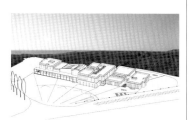

**Hashomer apartments and shops**
Tel Aviv, Israel
Completion date: 2004

236

# Appendix

# Biography

Nili Portugali was born in Haifa, Israel, in 1948. She is a lecturer at the Bezalel Academy of Art & Design, Architectural Department, Jerusalem, and a practicing architect working in Israel for more than 30 years.

Her work has focused on both practice and theory, and is tightly connected to the Phenomenological-Holistic School of Thought.

Her firm is engaged in a variety of projects in architecture, urban design, landscape design and interior design in unique areas of historic or environmental sensitivity including public buildings, residential and mixed developments and private houses.

## Education

Technion Institute of Technology, Department of Architecture, Haifa, Israel, 1968–70.
Architectural Association School of Architecture (AA), London, 1970–73.
AA Diploma, 1973.
Royal Institute of British Architects (RIBA) Exams, part 1 and 2, 1973.
University of California, Berkeley, California, 1979 to 1981. Postgraduate studies in architecture and Buddhist studies.
Center for Environmental Structure, Berkeley, California. Research work with Christopher Alexander. Topics of research: the nature of spatial order, the phenomena of colors, simulation of design processes, site plan for Shorashim community village, Israel, 1979–81.

## Teaching

School for Environmental Design, Tel Aviv, 1985/86.
Bezalel Academy of Art & Design, Jerusalem, Department of Architecture, 1983 to this day. Teaching courses: holistic-phenomenological approach to architecture in theory and practice; the foundations of harmony in architecture; the phenomena of colors.

## Competition awards and entries

The Sephardic Central Synagogue, Hadera – first prize.
Residential neighborhood, Rishon Lezion – first prize.
Center for the Israeli Defense Army Veterans, Ramat Gan – first prize.
Residential houses in community villages (ideas competition) – purchase prize.
Memorial Site for The Fallen Intelligence Servicemen – purchase prize.
Civic center in Or Akiva.
Senior-citizens day center in Eilat.
Central city library in Haifa.
The Israel National War Memorial Center, Mount Eitan, Jerusalem.
Jewish comprehensive school in Berlin.
Student dormitories of Technion Institute of Technology, Haifa
Senior-citizens day center in Hadera.
"A building of good quality", Tuch residence, Jerusalem.

## Exhibitions

Linz, Austria: *The Timeless Way of Things*, with Christopher Alexander and Artemis Anninou, The Center for Environmental Structure, 1981.
Dizengoff Center, Tel Aviv: *40 under 40*, 1986.
The Israeli Architectural Association, Tel Aviv; Bezalel Academy of Art & Design, Jerusalem; Technion Institute of Technology, Haifa; City Museum, Rishon Lezion; City Hall, Jerusalem: competition entries, 1982 to this day.
Conference Center, Tel Aviv: *Conservation of Buildings and Sites in Israel*, 1992.
The Van Leer Institute, Jerusalem: *Heritage and Conservation*, 1994.
UIA World Congress of Architecture, Barcelona, Spain, 1996.
The Third Biennale for Architecture, Sao Paulo, Brazil, 1997.
The First Biennale for Architecture, Israel, 2000.

Jehoshua Park, Tel Aviv: *Public Buildings for the Year 2000*, 1999.

Israeli Architectural Association, Tel Aviv: *Community and Cultural Centers*, 2000.

City Hall, Tel Aviv: *Future Development Projects in the City of Jaffa*, 2000.

Maduradam, Holland: *Mini Israel*, 2000.

Mini Israel Park, Latrun: permanent exhibition.

The Forth Biennale for Architecture, Israel, 2004.

Biennale di Venezia – 9th International Architecture Exhibition, 2004.

Artists Gallery, Ein Hod: *Art in Architecture or Architecture as Art?*, 2004.

UIA World Congress of Architecture, Istanbul, 2005.


**Selected public lectures**

International Conference on Urban Rehabilitation and Renewal, Jerusalem, 1985.

International Conference on Heritage and Conservation, Jerusalem, 1986.

International Conference on Housing and Rehabilitation Services for the Aging, Jerusalem, 1987.

International Conference on Women Equality and Democracy, Creation, which Creates the World, Ben-Gurion University, Beer-Sheba, 2000.

Conference on Housing and Design, Hamacabia Conference Center, Ramat Gan, 2001.

Conference on The Sight of Sound, a Conjunction of Visual Arts, Music and Science, Bezalel Academy of Arts & Design, Jerusalem, 2002.

Conference on the Education of Architecture in Israel, Council for Higher Education in Israel, 2002.

Technion Institute of Technology, Haifa; Bezalel Academy of Art & Design, Jerusalem; Tel Aviv Museum of Modern Art; Bugrashov Art Gallery; Holon College of Design; Tsavta House, Haifa; The Kibbutz Center, Tel Aviv; Efal Educational Center, 1985 until today.

Motar (professional journal on the arts) Conference on the Object and its Meaning in the Arts, Tel Aviv University, Faculty of Arts, 2004.

Lecture on the holistic approach to architecture, its implementation in own work, in relation to the cultural and physical context of the place: The Van Leer Institute, Jerusalem, 2004; Bait Ariela city central library, Tel Aviv (2004); The Architectural Association House, Jaffa (2005).

UIA World Congress of Architecture, Istanbul, 2005.


**Film bibliography**

Israel Television BC Channels 1; 2; 33.

*Jewish Culture*, 1988: on the Sephardic Central Synagogue, Hadera.

*Art and Culture*, 1990: on the buildings and the design approach of Nili Portugali.

*Good Morning Israel*, 1993: on the music library in the central city library in Tel Aviv.

*What's New in Ramat Gan*, 1996: on the Ohel Shem school and community library, Ramat Gan.

*Design*, 1996: on the music center and library in Tel Aviv.

*Women Magazine*, 1998: on the senior-citizens day center in Tel Aviv.

*What's New in Tel Aviv*, 2000: on the music center and library in Tel Aviv.

*Theatre Café*, 2000: on the Relationship between the creation process and the place of creation in the arts.

*On Jewish Culture and Tradition*, 2002: on the design approach and working process of Nili Portugali, in relation to tradition.

UIA World Congress of Architecture, Istanbul, Turkey, 2005: multimedia show on the holistic approach to architecture.


**Professional affiliations**

Member of the committee of the Jehoshua Rabinowitch Foundation for the Arts and Literature, Tel Aviv, 1990–92.

Member of the committee for the authorization of schools of architecture in Israel of the Council for Higher Education, 1997–99.

Member of the Public Council for Research and Development for Educational and Welfare Institutions, 2000–04.

External examiner for MA thesis at the Technion Institute of Technology, Faculty of Architecture, Haifa, Israel.

# Writings by Nili Portugali

## Books and catalogues

"A Holistic Approach to Physical Planning, its Application in the Creation of an Organic Order as Implemented in the Design of Two Public Buildings", in: Turner, Michael (ed.), *The Jerusalem Paper No. 2, An International Workshop on Heritage and Conservation,* Jerusalem, 1986.

"A Holistic Approach to Planning, its Implementation in Ramat Gan Neighborhood Renewal", in: *An International* Conference on *Urban Revitalization,* Jerusalem, 1986 (abstracts).

"A Holistic Approach to Physical Planning, as Implemented in the Design of a Day Center for the Aged in Tel Aviv", in: *International Conference on Housing and Services for the Aging,* Jerusalem, 1987 (abstracts).

"The Music Center and Library, 26 Bialik Street, a Dialogue Between a New Building and the Historical Environment", in: Widrich, Shulamit, and Regev-Yarkoni, Hadas, *Bialik Street, Spin, Spirit and Shape,* Tel Aviv, 2004.

"A Holistic Approach to Architecture – The Interrelation between the Creation Process and the Spirit of the Place: A Case Study, Israel", in: *UIA World Congress of Architects,* Istanbul, 2005 (abstracts).

## Periodicals and researches

"Re-planning of Moshav Bnei Re'em Center", 1983 (research).

"Re-planning of Moshav Neveh Mivtah Center", 1983 (research).

"A Memorial Site for the Fallen Members of the Israeli Intelligence Corps, Glilot", *Architecture in Israel,* 1982/83.

"A Different Approach to Planning and Building – Its Implementation in Cooperative Settlements", *Hamoshavim, the Bulletin of the Agricultural Family,* December 1984, January 1985.

"Architecture as an Organic Process, its Implementation in Planning Buildings and Their Outdoors", *Hamoshavim,* April 1985.

"Architecture as an Organic Process", *Mivnim,* no. 39, November 1985.

"Ramat Amidar Renewal Project, Ramat Gan" (research), *Tvai, Architecture and Town Planning,* no. 22, 1982.

"The Apartment Building and Public Housing", *Hakablan Vehaboneh,* March 1988.

"Senior-Citizens Day Center, Rashi Street Tel Aviv", *Mivnim,* no. 70, July 1988; *Israeli Architecture,* no. 4, April 1988.

"A Holistic Approach to Planning and Building – Its Expression in the Planning of Two Public Buildings at the Heart of Tel Aviv", *Kav,* no. 9, January 1989; *Mivnim,* no. 80.

"Givatayim Post Office", *Mivnim,* no. 91, April 1990.

"Synagogue Hadera", *Globes Design,* no. 6, June 1990.

"'Villas City' Rishon Lezion", *Globes Design,* no. 7, September 1990.

"The Eyes of the Building – An Approach to Architectural Planning", *Studio,* no. 18, January 1991.

"Music Library, Beit Ariella Tel Aviv"; *Globes Design,* no. 11, December 1991; *Mivnim,* no. 108, September 1991.

"Portugali Residence, Zichron Ya'akov", *Globes Design,* no. 19, December 1993.

"Shutz Residence, Jerusalem", *Globes Design,* no. 20, March 1994.

"A Different Approach to Planning, its Implementation in the Planning of Communal Settlements, Do Your Own House System", *Mivnim,* no. 61, September 1987; *Alef-Alef, the Architectural Associaton of Israel Bulletin,* November 1994.

"Ramat Gan City Hall", *Mivnim,* no. 138, March 1994; *Globes Design,* no. 22, November 1994.

"Ben-Avraham Residence – Zichron Ya'akov", *Globes Design,* no. 24, April 1995.

"Ma'alot Tarshiha Market", *Mivnim,* no. 150, March 1995.

"Beit Tsevet, *Globes Design,* no. 25, July 1995.

"The Israel National War Memorial Center, Mount Eitan, Jerusalem", *Mivnim*, no. 169, October 1996; *Globes Design*, 30, December 1996; *Studio*, no. 72, May/June 1996; *Hatach Alef-Alef, The Architects Association of Israel Newsletter*, no. 50, October 1996.

"Site Plan for Mevaseret Yerushalayim", 1986 (research).

"Moshav Shorashim", *Mivnim*, no. 107, December 1996.

"A Dynamic Planning Process for a Metropolis – A New Approach", *Mivnim*, no. 171, December 1996.

"Israel Architects Association is Enslaved", *Mivnim*, no. 173, February 1997.

"The Architectural Association, is it Enslaved or Have the Freedom to Judge?", *Engineers Architects and Technologists*, June 1997.

"Neighborhood Center Ramot", *Globes Design*, no. 15, December 1995; *Mivnim*, no. 60, August 1997.

"Ohel Shem Library Ramat Gan", *Globes Design*, no. 31, march 1997; *Mivnim*, no. 153, June 1995; *Mivnim*, no. 177, June 1997; *Globes Design*, no. 26, October 1995; *Engineers, Architects and Technologists*, September 1997.

"A Model for the Planning Process", *Mivnim*, October 1997.

"Lofts in Jaffa", *Globes Design*, no. 34, December 1997.

"Music Center and Library Bialik Square Tel Aviv", *Mivnim*, no. 140, May 1994; *Globes Design*, no. 36, June 1998; *Mivnim*, no. 194, November 1998; *Engineers and Architects*, September/October 1998.

"Yefet Hatzorfim Development Project, Jaffa", *Mivnim*, April 1999.

"Student Dormitories, Technion Haifa", *Mivnim*, no. 225, June 2001.

"The Status of the Architect in Israel. A Mirror for a Cultureless Society", *Perspectiva, Architects Association Bulletin*, July 2001.

"A Unique Approach to Architectural Planning, its Implementation in Residential Neighborhoods in Israel", *Hakablan Vehabone*, October 2001.

"David Residence, Zichron Ya'akov", *Ma'ariv Design*, no. 43, June 2000, *Ma'ariv Design*, no. 56, October 2002.

"Hibat Zion Synagogue, Jerusalem", *Mivnim*, no. 238, September/October 2002.

"A Holistic Approach to Planning and its Implementation in Educational, Cultural and Welfare Buildings", *Hakablan Vehabone*, December 2002.

"Kibbutz Ma'agan Michael", *Ma'ariv design*, no. 41, February 2000; *Hakablan Vehabone*, October 2001; *Building and Architecture*, no. 84, 2003.

"Hashomer Apartments and Shops, Tel Aviv", *Globes Design*, no. 37, August 1998; *Mivnim*, no. 242, May/June 2003; *Hakablan Vehabone*, September 2004; *Mivnim*, December 2004.

"A Holistic Approach to Architecture and its Implementation in the Physical and Cultural Context of the Place", *Alpayim, A Multidisciplinary Publication for Contemporary Thought and Literature*, no. 29, 2005.

"A Human Environment", *Mivnim*, no. 203, August 1999.

"Apartment Buildings, A Different Approach to Planning", *Mivnim*, no. 56.

"A Different Approach to Planning, its Expression in Build Your House (Ideas competion entry)", *Binyan Diur*, no. 10.

"The Hypochracy of the Post-Zionist Artists and Architects", *Perspectiva, the Architectural Association Bulletin*, no. 20.


**Daily press**

"Contemporary Architecture is Back to Facism", *Ha'aretz*, 20 January 1988.

"The Failure of Modernism", Ha'aretz, 21 July 1994.

"Rothschild Boulevard is a Barren Competition", *Friday Globes*, 30 June 1995.

"There are Prophets in Our City, The Import of Architects from Overseas", *Ha'ir*, 23 May 1996.

"The Synagogue as a Refinery, the Tel Aviv University New Synagogue", *Ha'aretz*, 17 December 1996.

"Building Rights for Preservation (Preservation Policy in Tel Aviv)", *Ha'ir*, 2 February 1998.

"The Correct Poster – the Competition Committee for the Independence Day Poster, and about Competition Committees in General", *Ha'aretz*, 1 January 1997; *Ha'aretz*, 5 April 1998.

"There is Another Religion, the Connection between Religion and Creative Freedom", *Ha'aretz*, 2 June 1998.

"Not All Houses Were Born Equal", *Ha'aretz*, 31 August 1999.

"Where should Architecture to be Studied", *Ha'aretz*, 31 October 1999.

"The Rabin Surplus Fortress", *Ha'aretz*, 30 July 2000.

"Equality of Opportunities and Qualities, versus Quantitative and Formal Uniformity", *Hadaf Hayarok Supplement, Ma'ariv*, 4 May 2000.

"We are both from the same Pattern", *Kav Lamoshav Supplement, Ma'ariv*, 29 May 2000.

"The Systematic Destruction of the Public Space, Kikar Hamedina", *Ha'aretz*, 5 December 2001.

"The Support of Lecturers and Academicians in the Phenomena of Subordination, is more Dangerous than the Insubordination Itself", *Ha'aretz*, February, 2002.

# Writings on Nili Portugali

**Books and catalogues**

"Citizens Day Center, Welfare Offices Center, Shutz Residence", in: *Young Architecture in the Basement, 40 under 40*, Tel Aviv 1986 (exhibition at the Dizengoff Center, Tel Aviv).
"Hadera Synagogue", in: *The Structure of Synagogues In Israel, 1948–1993*, Jerusalem 1993 (exhibition at Bezalel Gallery, Jerusalem).
*Dictionnaire de l'architecture du XXe siècle*, Paris, 1996, p. 720.
*Merhav 2000 – The First Biennale for Architecture in Israel*, Tel Aviv, 1997.
*The Third Bienal Internacional De Arquitetura De Sao Paulo Brazil*, Sao Paulo, 1997, p. 31.
"International Center for the Study of Bird Migration Project", in: Leshem, Yosi, and Bahat, Ofer, *Flying with the Birds*, Tel Aviv, 1999, p. 220 (drawing by Nili Portugali).
"Illustration of a Design Process", *in:* Alexander, Christopher, *The Nature of Order*, Berkeley, 2003 (book 2), 2004 (book 3). Book 2, p. 62 bottom left (drawing by Nili Portugali); book 3, p. 351 (Moshav Shorashim, Galilee, Israel).
"The Music Center and Library, 26 Bialik Street Tel Aviv", in: Shapira, Yoni, *Mini Israel Guide,* Herzliya, 2003.
"The Jewish Comprehensive School Competition in Berlin", in: *Realisierungswettbewerb, Grundschule der Jüdischen Gemeinde zu Berlin*, Berlin, 1990.
"Nili Portugali the Architect, 26 Bialik Street, Tel Aviv", in: Widrich, Shulamit, and Regev-Yarkoni, Hadas, *Bialik Street, Spin, Spirit and Shape,* Tel Aviv, 2004.

**Periodicals**

"Moshav Shorashim" *Yarok Kachol Lavan*, no. 14.
"Music Library, Beit Ariella Tel Aviv", *Binyan Diur*, no. 36, February 1995; *Olam Haisha*, January 1988.
"The Scenery, is her Office", *Na'amat Monthly*, no. 112, January 1989.

"Exhibition on Preservation and Rehabilitation", *Engineers and Architectects Weekly*, December 1990.
"Portugali Residence, Zichron Ya'akov", *Binyan Diur*, no. 25, July/August/September 1992.
"Ramat Gan City Hall", *Binyan Diur*, no. 34, September/October 1995.
"Beit Tsevet", *Tsevet Newsletter*, 22 May 1995.
"Toch Residence Jerusalem", *Olam Haisha Design*, October 1997; *Binyan Diur*, no. 46, October/ November 1996.
"The Music of Architecture", *Israelal*, no. 78, March/ April 1998.
"Kibbutz Ma'agan Michael", *Bayit Vanoy*, no. 61, October/November 2001.
"Ben-Avraham Residence, Zichron Ya'akov", *Binyan Diur*, no. 33, August/September 1994; *Binyan Diur*, no. 25, July/August/September 1992; *Bayit Vanoy*, no. 55, October/November 2001.

**Daily press**

"Music Center and Library Tel Aviv", *Israeli Architecture*, no. 53, May 2003.
"Shutz Residence, Jerusalem", *Binyan Diur*, no. 11.
"Equality of Qualities instead of Formal Uniformity", *Al Ha'deshe Supplement*, 21 October 1985 (interview).
"The Portugali Case", *Bayit Plus, Monitin*, 1986.
"Young Architectects at Dizengoff Center, Tel Aviv", *Ha'ir*, 12 September 1986.
"Apartment House, Givatayim", *Ha'ir*, June 26, 1987.
"The Vision of Dreams And The Production of Concrete Boxes", *Ha'ir*, 29 April 1988 (interview).
"Villas City, Rishon Lezion", *Ma'ariv Monthly, Tarbut Hadiur*, July 1998; *Rehovot-Rishon Lezion paper*, 28 July 1988.
"Senior-Citizens Day Center, Tel Aviv", *Ha'ir*, 28 August 1984; *Ha'ir*, 28 December 1984; *Ma'ariv Tel Aviv*, 19 December 1986; *Ha'ir*, 9 June 1988; *Ma'ariv*, 24 June 1988; *Ha'aretz*, 19 July 1988; *Shishim Plus*, July 1988.

The opening ceremony of the senior-citizens day center, announcement from the mayor Mr. S. Lahat to the citizens, *The City Hall Brochure*, 26 June 1988.

"Rome is What It is Lacking, The Potbelly of the Architect, A Symposium, Museum of Modern Art, Tel Aviv", *Ha'ir*, 1 January 1989 (interview).

"Trying to Catch the Spirit of the Place", *Weekly Davar Supplement*, 1 January 1989.

"Neighborhood Center Ramot, Jerusalem", *Kol Ha'ir*, December 1986; *Jerusalem*, 26 February 1988; *Ha'aretz*, 8 March 1989.

"Toch House", *Tel Aviv*, May 1989.

"No Common Language, Exhibition on the City's Nucleus Projects", *Ha'aretz*, 7 June 1990 (interview).

"The Central Sephardi Synagogue, Hadera", *Hadashot Hadera*, 22 November 1987; *Hamodia*, 25 December 1987; *Davar*, 1 January 1988; *Hatzofe*, 11 January 1988; *Jerusalem Post*, 29 January 1988; *Hadashot Hadera*, 27 May 1988; *Natanya Weekly, Yediot Aharonot*, 1 July 1988; *Photo Florida News USA*, 9 October 1989; *Hashomron News*, 19 January 1990; *Yediot Aharonot*, 16 March 1990; *Ha'aretz*, 12 March 1991.

"Hibat Zion Synagogue, Jerusalem", *Ha'aretz*, 12 March 1991.

"Mobile Market, Ramt-Gan", *Tel Aviv*, 5 May 1991, *Ha'aretz*, 8 May 1991.

"Post Office Givatayim", *Ma'ariv Tel Aviv*, 10 May 1991.

"A Gate to Israel, A Black Island in the Sea", *Ha'ir*, 10 January 1992 (interview).

"Music Library Beit Ariella, Tel Aviv", *Ha'aretz*, 13 January 1993; *Yediot Aharonot Plus*, 31 January 1993; *Index Local Paper*, January 1994; *Hatzofe*, 13 January 1994; *Emtzah Hashavua*, January 1994; *Telegraph*, 14 January 1994.

"Ramat Gan City Hall", *Al Hamishmar*, 13 January 1994; *Yediot Aharonot*, 16 January 1994; *Ha'aretz*, 10 February 1994.

"The Manshia Plan", *Ha'ir*, 1 January 1995 (interview).

"Build Your Own House in the Kibbutz", *Al Hamishmar*, 8 April 1995 (interview).

"How to Detonate Kikar Atarim", *Weekly Ha'aretz Supplement*, 26 May 1995 (interview).

"Beit Tsevet', *Ha'ir*, 9 June 1995.

"The Center for the Study of Bird Migration, Latrun", *Jerusalem Newspaper*, 3 October 1995.

"A Ceramic Heart, Construction in Tel Aviv", *Zman Tel Aviv*, 17 November 1995 (interview).

"West Yefet Hatzorfim Development, Jaffa", *Zman Tel Aviv*, 9 February 1996.

"Ohel Shem Library, Ramat Gan", *Hashavua, Givatayim and Ramat Gan*, 30 December 1996.

"From the Kitchen to the Bedroom in Three Steps", *Weekly Ha'aretz Supplement*, 18 April 1997 (interview).

"The Leading Architects", *Ha'ir*, 22 October 1997.

"Hashomer Apartments and Shops", *Ha'ir*, 22 May 1998.

"Living in the Space", *Bait Vagan Supplement, Ma'ariv*, 19 October 1999.

"Hadera City Hall", *This Week in Hadera*, 9 February 2000.

"The Holistic Organic Approach in Nili Portugali's Architecture", *Itzuv Aher Supplement, Ha'aretz*, 10 January 2001.

"Building from the Site", *Bayit Vagan Supplement, Ma'ariv*, 14 August 2001.

"Kibbutz Ma'agan Michael", *Hadaf Hayarok Supplement*, Ma'ariv, 5 July 2001; *Bayit Vagan Supplement, Ma'ariv*, 14 August 2001.

"Behind the Beauty and Harmony there are Facts", *Textura, Architectural Magazine, Globes*, 7 February 2002.

"First of All, A Glass Jacuzzi, What is A Dream House", *Weekly Ha'aretz Supplement*, 9 July 2003 (interview).

"Music Center and Library, Tel Aviv", *Ha'ir*, 24 November 1989; *Ha'ir*, 26 November 1993; *Ha'aretz*, 10 February 1994; *Zman Tel Aviv*, 8 December 1995, 28 November 1996; *Tel Aviv*, 26 December 1996; *Camelot*, January 1997; *Ha'ir*, 21 March 1997; *The Tel Aviv Municipality, Arnona booklet Tel Aviv*, 1998; *Kolbo*, 5 November 2004.

**On the internet (by Nili Portugali)**

www.umbauverlag.com/Neue_Dateien/Holistic Approach.pdf
www.icl.org.il/Portugali.asp
www.archijob.co.il (articles)
www.uia-atlas.org (projects)
www.archijob.co.il/aj-projects/pr22/main.hml
www.kibbutz.org.il/orchim/041006_nili_portugali.htm
www.Intbau.org/essay11.htm
www.niliportugali.com

**On the internet (on Nili Portugali)**

http://www.umbau-verlag.com/Essays/NiliPortugali.html
http://www.architectureweek.com/2005/0202/culture.html. "More Building Culture – A Holistic Approach to Architecture" (article)
http://www.architectureweek.com/2001/0404/design_1-1html
http://www.architectureweek.com/2005/0406/culture_1-1.html
http://www.architectureweek.com/2001/0905/culture_2-1.html
www.tarbut-now/newsletters/200509/200509.html

# Credits

**Photography**

Nili Portugali
Adiel Portugali
Rami Arnold
Amit Geron
Ran Erda

**Computer work**

Lili Leikind
Dan Marcus
Kineret Avraham

All architectural drawings, illustrations, 3D simulations and photographs belong to Nili Portugali.

**References**

Alexander, Christopher, S. Ishikawa, M. Silverstein, M. Jacobson, I. Fiksdahl-King, S. Angel, *A Pattern Language*, New York, 1977.
Alexander, Christopher, *The Timeless Way of Building*, New York, 1979.
Alexander, Christopher, *The Nature of Order*, Berkeley, 2002–04.
His Holiness the Dalai Lama, *The Joy of Living and Dying in Peace*, New Delhi, 1997.
Grabow, Stephen, *Christopher Alexander, The Search for a New Paradigm in Architecture*, Boston, 1983.
Herrigel, Eugen, *Zen and the Art of Archery*, New York, 1964.

# Acknowledgements

I would like to thank the people whose work made a special contribution to this book. To Hedva Ehrlich for translating and editing the text and adding her unique professional input in the production of the book as a whole.

To my husband Juval and to my children Odelia and Adiel for contributing their academic knowledge, work and creative ideas along the way.

To Gleb Shebaleb, my employee in the past, for his outstanding watercolor paintings and 3D digital models of the following projects presented in the book: The Israel National War Memorial Center, lofts, music center and library, International Center for the Study of Bird Migration and Field Study School, cafeteria pavilion, Tselermayer residence, cultural center and library, commercial and leisure center, central city library and resource center, residential neighborhood in a kibbutz.

And last but not least, to the sponsors and people whose kind financial support made it possible for me to publish this book:
my parents Yona and Shmuel Kahan,
The Jehoshua Rabinowitch Foundation for the Arts,
The Israel National Lottery Council for the Arts.

*Nili Portugali, watercolor, 1980, seminar on colors, University of California, Berkeley.*